ZLONK! ZOK! ZOWIE!

The Subterranean Blue Grotto Essays on Batman '66 – Season One

Second Edition

Edited By

Jim Beard

with Rich Handley

ZLONK! ZOK! ZOWIE!
The Subterranean Blue Grotto Essays
on Batman '66 – Season One

A Becky Books Production

Cover design by Sean E. Ali

Interior layout and formatting by Maggie Ryel

ISBN: 9798474623429

Crazy Eight Press is an imprint of ComicMix LLC.

For information address Crazy 8 Press at the official Crazy 8 website:
www.crazy8press.com

Second edition

For the Little Woman, who had a crush on Burt Ward's Robin as a child and his action figure as an adult.

Jim Beard, Editor

TABLE OF BAT-CONTENTS

TABLE OF BAT-CONTENTS

ZLONK!

Holy Sideways Sequel, Batman!

An Introduction by Jim Beard

"For One Desperate Decade the Bat-Signal Blazed in the Sky! For Ten Yawning Years the Hot-Line Remained Unanswered! Where Is the Sequel to *Gotham City 14 Miles?* Not Even Jim Knows!"

Hmm, that makes for a fairly fun parody of the deathless prose on the cover of *Batman* #184 (though out of date if you're reading this later than 2020), but perhaps a better self-lambasting could be had in paraphrasing *Batman* #183's cover text:

"Holy Prolific Procrastination! What's the *Real* Reason Jim's Been Goofing Off? The Telltale Clue Is in This Introduction!"

Now, settle down; I'm not going to make you solve riddles or dissect the punchlines to jokes or anything like that—but I will try to play it straight with you and explain what this book is you're holding in your Bat-gloved mitts, and how it happened.

So, you're here because you're a fan of the 1966-'68 *Batman* TV series, or maybe the Silver Age Batman comic character, or possibly even because you enjoyed my 2010 tome titled *Gotham City 14 Miles: 14 Essays on Why the 1960s Batman TV Series Matters*, or a combination thereof. Okay, that's covered. Now, *I'm* here because of similar reasons: I dig the show and the character, and I'm the creator-editor of *Gotham City 14 Miles*. In addition, I am also the possessor of the unswerving belief that there are just not enough books about the show, which hasn't really changed at all for me ("unswerving") since 2009.

Once published, *Gotham City 14 Miles* garnered near-universal acclaim for its passion for its subject matter and for being the first true examination of the show from multiple angles, much to my utter delight and eternal gratitude. See, I felt I was finally justified in my love for *Batman* '66 and my faith in its true worth in cultural history when I heard about the reviews and the interest the book had produced. Believe me when I say it was a good feeling.

Then I received calls for more. What could I do? *Gotham City 15 Miles? Even More Miles to Gotham? Are We in Gotham Yet? You Should Have Gone When We Were Still at the Batcave?*

Suffice to say, a sequel was a daunting proposition, because I really felt like we'd mined for gold, struck it, and probably tapped out that vein. A few years after publication—true story—I did go down the road of examining the possibility of a sequel called...wait for it...*Gotham City Plans and Views*, but after some disappointing rounds of essay topic pitching, I closed it down for good. To me, G*otham City 14 Miles* was a done-in-one, and anything we'd do to sequelize it would just come up short of the high-water mark we'd set with the original. Or so I thought.

Flash forward to 2018. During a long drive from Northwest Ohio to Atlanta, Georgia, I conceived of an idea while listening to the 1966 *Batman* feature film soundtrack—how about a *sideways* sequel?

Sure, there have been quite a few reviews throughout the past fifty years of *Batman*'s episodes, most of them online in blogs and what-have-you, and many of them have been great and fun, but my thought was to not only bring in an even higher caliber of writers for reviews, but to inspire each one of them to find a *hook* to skewer each episode, reel it in, and hang it up for everyone to see and be illuminated. It hadn't been done before, in my estimation, just like

Gotham City 14 Miles had forged a new path back in 2010, and boy! if I could get a lot of the same writers back, plus some new scribes, what a gas it'd be—a "sideways sequel" to please everyone. Not only that, but groovy and gear, too.

And that's the book you're looking at right now, the one Alfred just handed to you off a silver tray with a glass of milk and some cookies.

What? Oh, the prolific procrastination? Yeah, that. Y'see, this book took about two years to come to fruition, much longer than I'd expected, and for that I apologize to you and to my writers and artists. John Lennon said "Life's what happens to you while you're busy making other plans," and man, did he ever nail that one down tight. In the meantime between this project's conception and birth, I experienced a life-changing event of seismic magnitude, one that—coupled with my infamous procrastination—bogged down this little beauty for far too long...but with a little help from my friends, it's here now and hopefully once you reach the last page you'll feel it's all been worth the wait.

As always, let me know what you think. Volume Two will be out in 2030, and Volume Three in 2040.

Jim Beard
The Batcave
February 2020

ZOK!

Another Cold, January Evening in Gotham City...

"Hi Diddle Riddle/Smack in the Middle"

By Jim Beard

Lee Baldwin closed the garage door over his station wagon and wondered for the hundredth time since he left work why it was always a Wednesday when his boss asked him to work late. Finding no answers in the chilly, mid-January air, he turned to trudge through the snow to his house and up the back stairs.

Just barely setting a toe on the back porch, he heard the pounding of feet in the house, and before he knew it the door had been flung open to reveal the beaming, cherubic face of his eight-year-old son, Larry.

"Mom went to Mrs. Johnson's!" the boy exclaimed. "You wanna watch TV with me tonight?"

"Can I at least come in and get warm first?" Lee asked, knocking the snow from his shoes and setting his briefcase down. It wasn't exactly what he had in mind, *television*, but for some reason the kid was excited about it.

Still smiling, the boy backed up to give his father room. "There's a new one on tonight at 7:30!"

Lee shrugged off his coat and laid it over a kitchen chair as he glanced at the clock on the wall—6:35pm. Why was his boss such a slavedriver? "New one? In January? I thought you watched *Lost in Space* on Wednesdays?"

From out of nowhere a copy of *TV Guide* was thrust in his face. Eva Gabor and Eddie Albert flashed their teeth at him on the cover. Calmly and without anger, he reached out to move the little magazine and his son's hand holding it to a more easily digestible distance. "We already watch *Green Acres*, son—and that's not on Wednesdays."

"No, Dad!" Larry protested, flipping open the *TV Guide* and once again thrusting it into his father's vision. "This! Right here! *Look!*"

Lee looked at the page where his son's finger pointed. There, at the bottom half of A-45, was a "TV Guide Close Up" spotlighting—he squinted over his glasses—'Hey Diddle Diddle' and below the words a photo of two masked people sitting in what looked like an oddball double-cockpit of a jet...or a spaceship?

"It's *Batman*," said his son, as if it was the most obvious thing ever in the entire world.

He looked closer, saw the name of the new program finally. Good Lord, it *was* Batman.

Wait... Batman? Really?

But—hadn't he read Batman comic books when he was a kid, about the age of his son? Hadn't he enjoyed them back then? Even traded a few other comics for Batman's? Lee remembered summer evenings after coming in from playing when he would sit with his younger brother and read to him from the stories...they'd both loved that. Batman was fun, colorful—exciting.

His stomach growled to bring him out of his momentary reverie. Looking up over the open *TV Guide* at Larry's face he saw—what? Excitement. That's what it was. The same excitement that was probably all over his own face when he read one of those comic books back in the day.

"Can I eat first, you think?" he asked his son, trying to keep a smile off his own face. "We have almost an hour before this goofy thing's on...probably some TV dinners around here somewhere."

Larry just stood there, smiling and slowly nodding his head.

"Batman, huh?"

"Batman," his son replied.

"Okay...Batman it is."

Bellies full and appetites sated, they reconvened in the den in front of the family's not-such-a-bad-size RCA black-and-white television, Lee in his La-Z-Boy and Larry on the floor with an array of colorful comic books splayed out before him.

"Hey, are we watching the show or reading, sport?"

"Quiet, Dad!" the boy yelped, pointing at the TV. "It's on!"

The title card on the screen proclaimed "BATMAN IN COLOR" and he felt his face get warm when he heard his son sigh quietly, momentarily hanging his head over his comics. Then, for the next few minutes until the first commercial, they were bombarded with a series of characters, locations, exploding cakes, riddles, and even, of all things, a *narrator* urging them to get into the spirit of the thing. Incredibly, he found himself thinking over it all instead of reaching for the newspaper.

It was an odd show, to be sure; like nothing else Lee'd seen. Kind of broad and simple, childlike even, but packed full of things hurtling at the viewer in quick succession. And hadn't some of the actors seemed familiar, like the butler and the aunt? He recognized old Neil Hamilton as the police commissioner, but that Adam West was new to him. Good-looking guy with a good voice. But that kid? Burt something? Hardly the Dick Grayson he remembered from the comics—this guy had to be twenty if he was a day, but he ran around like a twelve-year-old.

"The Riddler's in this comic I borrowed from Mikey," his son told him, holding up a book with a garish hot pink cover and Batman and Robin trying to punch a whirling green figure in a mask. The Riddler? It wasn't coming to him; not one he recalled. The Joker, the

Penguin, the Cat Lady or something, but no Riddler.

"Mikey's older brother said he's from a long time ago," Larry continued, "like when you were a kid."

Speaking of Batman and Robin—the show was devoid of them so far, except for the cartoon credit sequence after the first few scenes. Now *those* were the characters he remembered. And that theme song! His son apparently ate it all up, but he had to suppress a chuckle at the nuttiness of it all: "*Na-na-na-na-na-na-Batman*"? Who were they trying to kid?

When the show returned, it offered up the title character and his sidekick in the flesh, and, he had to admit, a steady stream of electrical excitement. The cave! The car! It even had fire coming out the backside! "Gotham City 14 Miles"? Sure, why not? All bets were off. Lee sat back in the recliner and let it happen as his son pounded the carpet and cheered at the masked figures and their souped-up jalopy.

He'd say it again: Like nothing he'd watched before on the ol' idiot box.

The breakneck pace continued through an interesting scene in the commissioner's office—Robin seemed to be the smart one with answers to the riddles, a fact the boy didn't miss.

"Boy, Robin's so cool, Dad!"

From there, it got a bit goofier as the duo climbed up a building and Batman cautioned his sidekick about "pedestrian safety" right after using a laser beam on some bars over a window. His son took it seriously, but Lee himself tried not to chuckle. It was a comedy, right? Or what did they call it now? "Camp"? Is that what they were watching? He couldn't quite get a lock on it, but maybe it didn't matter; there was something about a lawsuit from the Riddler and nobody was allowed to catch their breath.

He did recognize Frank Gorshin as the bad guy in a bright green topcoat with question marks all over it. Gorshin was also a comedian of sorts, an impressionist, and he remembered him from *The Ed Sullivan Show* and a recent *Combat!* episode.

And then there was the girl.

Lee glanced at the *TV Guide* listing—she must be that Jill St.

John. A real looker—he was glad his wife wasn't home to see his reaction to her in that dress she wore at the discotheque. Wow. Batman looked only slightly fazed, probably because he couldn't see too well out of that mask. And suddenly he was...*dancing*?

Okay, something wasn't exactly kosher about it. He thought back to the comic books of his youth and the Batman stories he read. Were they that silly? Sure, they were *comic books* after all and crazy and colorful and fun; he even remembered something at one point about aliens, and there were Christmas stories and the villains always had goofy crimes and...

But Batman dancing?

"Aww, mush," Larry offered along with a razzberry, shaking his head and looking down at the comics and away from the screen while the hero and the gorgeous chick frugged or whatever the hell they were doing. Was that all it was to the boy, Lee wondered? A guy and a girl cuttin' a rug—just some stupid grown-up stuff? It was confusing, but—he had to admit it—entertaining.

Batman ended up drugged with orange juice and the Riddler tried to steal the "Batmobile," but the car had a mind of its own and saved itself! The villain went along on his warped way, though, and kidnapped the Boy Wonder right out from under Batman's pointy nose.

Before he knew it, it was all over. The episode ended on a cliffhanger with Robin about to be cut up with a scalpel and the overheated narrator telling them to come back *the very next day* for the conclusion?

Lee grabbed the *TV Guide* and turned to the Thursday listings—yep, there it was: *Batman* on again, same time and everything.

"Well, of all the nutty things..." He looked down at his son. "Whattaya think, champ? It's just like they used to do to us in the theaters on Saturdays when I was a kid."

Larry smiled and shrugged. "Groovy, Dad...I just wish we could see it in color."

He frowned and nodded as he got up from the chair to hide his chagrin from his son. "Yeah, sure—it was still fun, though, huh? You liked it?"

"Uh-huh! Can't wait until tomorrow!"

Sometimes—but not too often—the benefit of working late one day meant being able to go home early the next day. It was just what Lee had hoped for as he snatched up his late holiday bonus and sped off to complete his self-appointed task before his son got home from school on Thursday.

One large shout of "*Dad!*" from the den at roughly four o'clock told him he'd managed to really surprise the boy.

"Yes, Larry?" he asked as he stepped into the room. "You called, or rather bellowed?"

"What is *that*?" his son demanded, staring wide-eyed at him while pointing to the opposite end of the den.

"Well," said Lee matter-of-factly, "the manual says it's a new RCA Victor television featuring a Hi-Lite Tube with Perma Chrome, but maybe you'd better check it just to make sure."

Larry jumped up and down in place, ecstatic. "What? How? *Why*?"

His father smiled and shrugged. "What do you mean, sport? How else we gonna watch *Batman* tonight?"

Father and son sequestered themselves once more at 7:30, he in his La-Z-Boy and his son at a TV tray with a snack of Flings and Faygo Orange Pop, but as they got comfortable a feminine voice through a crack in the den's door intruded upon their wholly male sanctuary.

"Lee, what in the *world*...?" asked his wife, just returned from another sojourn to the ailing Mrs. Johnson's down the street. "Is—is that *new*?"

"Shh, Mom!" Larry cautioned. "Our show's on!"

Lee turned to his wife and waved her off with a grin. "Yeah, I'll explain later, honey—our show's on!"

"Okay, *kids*," said the departing voice. "Enjoy *The Munsters*!"

Father and son harrumphed together and turned their attention back to their new television—their new *color* television, to be precise.

And said color was glorious.

The recap of the previous day's episode leapt out of the screen at them with a rainbow palette—the Riddler's green suit, Robin's red and yellow, and Batman's odd blue-purple. Lee knew right then and there it was absolutely the right decision to get the new TV. The cartoon credits were wondrous and he regretted not being able to see Wednesday's installment in color.

Things rushed on, as before. He learned Batman's and Molly's dance was called the "Batusi," and he stole a quick look at the closed den door when Jill St. John's name was heralded during the opening shots. From there, he and Larry discovered the bad guy didn't want to cut Robin up, but apparently made an impression of his face.

"Why didn't he take off Robin's mask when he had the chance?" he asked his son.

Larry frowned at his father's ignorance. "He can't do *that*, Dad! It's *Robin*!" he argued, as if that explained everything that needed explaining.

Events grew more surreal, which was saying a lot for the show. Lee shook his head at Molly's dressing up as Robin, inwardly chortling that no one could mistake those curves for a young boy's body. Or even a twenty-year-old's. In a skewed answer to this thought, Jill St. John donned a Robin mask—from the impression, apparently—and she was suddenly the Ward guy!

"That's weird!" exclaimed Larry, and Lee could only agree. Moments later, Batman was hurtling down what looked more like a road in California than outside a major East Coast city, his Batmobile impressing both father and son again. It had an automatic revolving-turn thingamajig and drag parachutes and everything—Lee recalled a comic book story from his youth about a new Batmobile with a bunch of gadgets built in, but the one in the show beat all that.

The Riddler's car, on the other hand, was something of an antique, comparatively. It looked like an early '50s Rolls or a caddy, but it tooled right along with Batman in hot pursuit until a ray from the hero's car put the kibosh on it. The Riddler ran off, cackling joyfully as always, and then Molly wormed her way into the Batcave and to her death.

"Ha!" Larry laughed. "He said 'What a way to *go-go!*"—get it, Dad?"

Lee assured his son he most definitely "got it," but inwardly he was still off-kilter. He couldn't credit Jill St. John as Robin…but maybe he wasn't supposed to. Larry accepted it, though the show was aimed at kids…wasn't it? Still, it made him a little uncomfortable to see the actor mincing around like he was a girl just disguised as a boy, and thanked goodness again his wife wasn't around to see it. Bad enough *Larry* had to see it.

Batman managed to figure out where Robin was being kept despite the sidekick seemingly the clever one of the team. Then the action danced back over to the World's Fair pavilion of the, what were they? Moldavians? Was that some kind of in-joke, too? Lee's head swam a little, but he should've waited and saved his confusion for the next one-two punch the show delivered—and boy, did it.

The heroes dove into a fight with the Riddler's henchmen, and the sounds of their punches sprang up on the screen—literally. There was a KRUNCH! and a BAM! and what he thought might've been ZLONK!

What was a "zlonk," exactly?

"Man-o-man!" shouted Larry as he punched the air with every swing Batman and Robin took. Lee thought it all looked pretty fake—fists were miles away from jaws—but the boy was loving every second of it.

And admittedly, Lee was kind of enjoying it, too. It made him feel like…like he was reading comic books on his front porch back in the old neighborhood, and running around afterward with some other kids, acting it out.

The producers of the show were either certifiable or geniuses; he couldn't decide which.

When all the crooks were clobbered, the Caped Crusader went after Gorshin, who, in a mad rush to either kill his nemesis or die trying, apparently…died?

Larry appeared a little crestfallen. "Geez, I figured they'd take him to jail," he said quietly. "But he blew himself up!"

"I kinda doubt that, champ," Lee offered. "Although, maybe because he's not been around long, they thought they'd just get rid of him."

It sounded lame coming out of his mouth, but he couldn't remember any villains dying in the comics. Then again, it was 1966 and things may have changed.

Before they knew it, the episode was at its end and Bruce broke from his mooning over Molly—Lee couldn't really blame the guy—to help Robin with homework. It was at that moment that it hit him like a ton of bricks: It was all about a father and son. Dick Grayson was Bruce's Ward, but Bruce treated him like a son in every way. All the lessons and the encouragement and the worry when Robin was kidnapped; every bit of doubt he had about the show slipped away when he saw it as a great message about parents and their children. And wow, did the kids of the day need *that* message!

"Next week's gonna be the Joker, Dad!"

Larry's shout burst Lee's thought bubble and he turned to his son, smiling. "Now *there's* a crook I recognize!" he told him. "Well, I guess that means we need to watch it again, hmm?"

"Heck, yeah!" Larry exclaimed and jumped up to take his TV tray to the kitchen.

Lee watched his son go. "No regrets about missing *Lost in Space* and *The Munsters*?"

The boy kept on going, but answered over his shoulder. "Uh-uh! Batman's boss!"

Lee sat back in his recliner, spying Larry's comic books on the floor. Reaching for one, he flipped it open to the first page and ran his eyes over the colorful art and splashy text.

"I better do some catching up, then…"

Jim Beard became a published writer when he sold a story to DC Comics in 2002. Since that time he's written official Star Wars and Ghostbusters comic book stories and contributed articles and essays to several volumes of comic book history. His prose work includes the novella *Kolchak: The Last Tempataion*; co-editing and contributing to *Planet of the Apes: Tales From the Forbidden Zone*; a story for *X-Files: Secret Agendas; Gotham City 14 Miles*, a book of essays on the 1966 Batman TV series; *SGT. Janus, Spirit-Breaker*, a collection of pulp ghost stories featuring his Edwardian occult detective; *Monster Earth*, a shared-world giant monster anthology; and *Captain Action: Riddle of the Glowing Men*, the first pulp prose novel based on the classic 1960s action figure. Jim also currently provides regular content for Marvel.com, the official Marvel Comics website.

Look for Jim on Amazon at www.amazon.com/author/jimbeard, on Facebook at www.facebook.com/thebeardjimbeard, and on Twitter at @writerjimbeard.

ZLONK!

Tropes Abandoned, Tropes As Yet Unseen

"Fine Feathered Finks/The Penguin's a Jinx"

By Keith R.A. DeCandido

While *Batman* is best known for its campiness and goofiness, the show also indulged in satire on more than one occasion. While it wasn't a regular feature of the show, when they did delve into satire, it was often clever and biting. Probably the two most obvious (and strongest) examples are the commentary on the art world in "Pop Goes the Joker"/"Flop Goes the Joker" and the brilliant sendup of politics in "Hizzoner the Penguin"/"Dizzoner the Penguin." Plus there was the sendup of world politics in the feature film.

Their first shot at it, though, was in the very second episode, when "Fine Feathered Finks" introduces us to Warden Crichton.

The notion of prisoner's rights was still a relatively new—and controversial—one in 1966. Exactly one hundred years earlier, the Supreme Court ruled that prisoners have no Constitutional rights

(*Pervear v. Massachusetts*, 1866), but the combination of riots due to unsafe conditions in the 1950s (riots which continued for two decades, culminating in the brutal Attica riot of 1971) and the Civil Rights movement of the 1960s led to more and more advocacy and consideration for the rights of prisoners, as well as those accused of crimes. That 1866 decision was overturned in 1964 by the Supreme Court (unanimously) in *Cooper v. Pate*, establishing that prisoners did, in fact, have rights. Plus, of course, the very year that this episode aired also saw the landmark *Miranda v. Arizona* decision, which is why law-enforcement is obligated to read people their rights when they're arrested or questioned by police.

It was in this post-war era that the notion of prisons as institutions of correction rather than punishment came to prominence. The American Prison Association changed its name in 1954 to the American Correctional Association. More emphasis was placed on reform than on revenge.

Not everyone thought this was such a hot idea, or a workable one. *Batman* in particular was predicated on the notion of returning villains—Cesar Romero, Burgess Meredith, and Frank Gorshin each appeared several times in the first season, and Julie Newmar and Victor Buono would return after singular appearances—which required them *not* to reform. (The inability of these arch-villains to reform is actually a plot point in the second season's "Catwoman Goes to College"/"Batman Displays His Knowledge.")

And Lorenzo Semple Jr. takes every opportunity to make fun of Crichton's reforms. At least part of it the generally broad nature of the show in general, but still, Crichton is played as a figure of fun, for the most part, his reforms treated with disdain. Crichton himself keeps constantly referring to them as "progressive policies," making sure to emphasize that. Of course, it's one of the tropes of the show that everything is over-described, but this was only the second story—a lot of those tropes hadn't settled in yet. (Just as an example, Wayne Manor was actually just called "Wayne Manor," not "Stately Wayne Manor," though it was then described as the "stately home of Bruce Wayne.")

The policies themselves are actually pretty bizarre, also. When prisoners are about to be released (as Penguin is), they're allowed to wear their civilian garb, and they're also placed in a special cell that has a hidden camera. It's not very well hidden, as Penguin and his henchman (whose civilian garb includes a domino mask, just in case we weren't sure he was a bad guy) find it before they finish their conversation. It also reveals that Penguin hasn't reformed in the least, a revelation that leaves Crichton crestfallen.

This is hilarious on several levels, of course. The first is that we've only seen Crichton's reformist sensibilities for five seconds, and they've been trashed pretty thoroughly. Also, Crichton went to the trouble of taping Penguin, but he obviously hadn't watched the tape yet, making you wonder what he was waiting for. (Shouldn't he at the very least have taken a glance at it *before* he was helicoptered to police headquarters?)

Again, this was only the second story, but we were well on the way to the show's hallmark of showing that Batman is the only person equipped to deal with arch-criminals like the Penguin. The Gotham City Police are comically ineffective throughout the series run (as an example, it never occurs to Commissioner Gordon that Penguin might use a pseudonym to buy an umbrella shop, and he totally misses the bog-obvious "K.G. Bird" *nom du plume*), and places like here, as well as his subsequent appearances (particularly "The Greatest Mother of Them All"/"Ma Parker," where Parker took over the prison), Crichton is shown to be equally ineffective.

In a lot of ways, it's a narrative cheat. The show is called *Batman*, and that means that the person who must always save the day is, in fact, the Caped Crusader. But the show repeatedly hedged their bets by also making Batman by far the only competent person in all of Gotham City. Every other authority figure we meet is really terrible at their jobs. Two that recurred and were regularly seen to be imbeciles were Crichton and Mayor Linseed. The latter was replaced in "Nora Clavicle and the Ladies Crime Club" because his wife refused to cook or clean or wash his shirts until he appointed Clavicle to replace Gordon as police commissioner. He laments that he's worn the same shirt for weeks and hasn't had a decent meal in months. (Clavicle's platform is that women can run Gotham better than men, and if the mayor doesn't know how to operate a washing machine or get his staff to provide him with clean clothes and food, you can kinda see her point...) And Crichton's reforms are regularly lampooned and seen to be ineffective, which is necessary to keep the recurring villains coming back. In both these cases, it simplifies the task of the writers, because *of course* Batman has to be the one to maintain law and order, because if we left it to *these* garbanzos, the city would be doomed.

The biggest offenders, of course, are the two in the opening credits, Gordon and Chief O'Hara. The three seasons of *Batman* are a chronicle of the spectacular failures of the Gotham City Police Department.

In fact, in this episode—and also in the previous one, "Hi Diddle Riddle"/"Smack in the Middle"—is a piece of the opening formula that they dropped after this, but which shows up the GCPD's ineffectiveness. Most of the beginning of "Fine Feathered Finks" is what we're used to five decades later from the top of a *Batman* episode: a criminal does something, Gordon and O'Hara learn of it, they activate the bat-phone, Alfred answers it at Wayne Manor and interrupts Bruce Wayne and Dick Grayson in whatever they're doing and then, after making excuses to Aunt Harriet, answer the call and slide down the Batpoles.

All of that is present in this episode, but with one interesting variation: Gordon first asks for volunteers to take on the criminal *du jour*. The other cops all look away and Gordon concludes that he must, instead, use the red phone that sits under glass.

This notion was abandoned in fairly short order, as going forward, Gordon would simply say that there was only one man who could stop that week's villain and push the button on the phone.

That's one of many ways that you can tell this is an early episode, before they'd completely settled on all the formulae that would later come to define the program. For starters, as with "Hi Diddle Riddle," "Fine Feathered Finks" ended with a cliffhanger that seemed tacked-on and unnecessary—mainly because in the early days of the show, it was intended to be a one-hour drama. But when ABC gave it two half-hour slots in the same week, the cliffhanger format was inserted into the first episode, and incorporated into future scripts. The one here is particularly weird, as Batman's plan to figure out the clues on the Bat-brella are suddenly abandoned in favor of a plan to go to Penguin's umbrella shop as Bruce Wayne and plant a bug. Unfortunately, Penguin discovers the bug, and puts Bruce in a deathtrap that he has to escape in "The Penguin's a Jinx." And in another case of a trope not having settled yet, William Dozier's voiceover says to tune in tomorrow, "same time, same channel," with no bat-prefix yet.

Later cliffhangers would, for the most part, put Batman and Robin in danger rather than the former's secret identity, and also what's frustrating about this one is that it's so out of place. After he escapes the Penguin's clutches, Bruce returns to the Batcave as Batman and he and Robin then try to figure out what clues there are on the Bat-brella—just like they were going to do before they decided to bug the Penguin!

(And by the way, what's with doing warrantless eavesdropping on a private citizen? When the Dynamic Duo are meeting with Gordon and Crichton early on, Batman reminds Robin that Penguin served his time and is no longer to be considered a criminal—yet later on, he tries to bug the guy, which is illegal. Robin even declares that his saying Penguin should stay in jail past his sentence was a stupid thing to say, an unusually spot-on self-critique from the Boy Wonder.)

Another trope that this episode doesn't indulge in, surprisingly, is everyone knowing who Bruce Wayne (or, rather, "Millionaire Bruce Wayne"—many have joked that he was so specifically referred to thusly that his legal first name was actually "Millionaire," with "Bruce" as his middle name) is. Penguin doesn't recognize him as the famous philanthropist when he comes into the umbrella shop to get his father's prize umbrella repaired, though later on, Penguin will know exactly who Wayne is (notably in the feature film).

The Penguin's actual plan is clever, and this set the tone for a lot of the Penguin's appearances, as more than any of the others, he tended toward misdirection. Forming a security firm ("The Penguin Goes Straight"/"Not Yet, He Ain't"), becoming a filmmaker ("Penguin is a Girl's Best Friend"/"Penguin Sets a Trend"/"Penguin's Disastrous End"), running for mayor ("Hizzoner the Penguin"/"Dizzoner the Penguin"), opening a fancy restaurant ("The Penguin's Nest"/"The Bird's Last Jest")—all distractions from his real plan. This one is particularly subtle, as Penguin has no idea what criminal act to perform. So instead, he commits acts that seem like the structure for a crime, but with no actual crime, to wit, giving away gag umbrellas at a jewelry store, which he then declines the opportunity to rob. Then he leaves a big-ass umbrella in the middle of a street, with a tiny umbrella attached to it. But Batman is enough of a detective that he'll try to find clues anyhow, and with Penguin having bugged the Bat-brella, he can listen in. This is played for laughs, naturally, as Batman and Robin make leaps in logic that the Hungarian judge would give a 9.5, and the deductive process he uses could kindly be considered tortured. This is one case where the story might have worked better later when we've seen the Caped Crusader and the Boy Wonder stumble their way to figuring out an abstruse clue, and seeing it made fun of works even better. Of course, fifty-odd years on, we're all familiar anyhow...

Burgess Meredith does a simply superlative job here. One of the reasons why *Batman* was so successful was its villains. In particular, the "big four" of Cesar Romero, Julie Newmar, Frank Gorshin, and Meredith all threw themselves so totally into the parts they played. In this first appearance even more than his others, Meredith embodies the *faux* aristocratic air of the comics character.

In another case of lack of unexpected tropes, we don't once here the Penguin's trademark "Waugh! Waugh!" Meredith developed that in later appearances to cover his coughing. He had quit smoking, but the Penguin role required him to have his cigarette holder—lit, of course (yay 1966)—and he didn't want his coughing to muck up his dialogue, so he developed that signature noise to cover it.

Like many first-season episodes, Dozier had his writers mine the comics for story inspiration, mostly motivated by the rushed nature of that first season, slammed into production in January 1966. In this case, the story is inspired by the "Partners in Plunder" story in *Batman* #169 by Ed Herron, Sheldon Moldoff, & Joe Giella, which came complete with a giant umbrella in the middle of a Gotham City street. The big change was, instead of stealing a giant jeweled meteorite (which would be expensive to create), kidnapping a starlet (the much-easier-to-hire Leslie Parrish).

The starlet-kidnapping plot also provides us with one of the earliest examples of yet another of *Batman*'s classic tropes, the renaming of something real. Mostly the show did this with New York City locations and people (Short Island for Long Island, Spiffany's for Tiffany's, Governor Stonefellow and the aforementioned Mayor Linseed for Governor Rockefeller and Mayor Lindsay, and so on), and we get an early non-New York example here, as Dawn Robbins is in Gotham to do a photo shoot for *Funboy* magazine. Wah-hey!

The opening at Wayne Manor—which only occasionally related to the rest of the episode—had an interesting bit of foreshadowing for the feature film, as Dick Grayson is doing his French homework. He's struggling with conjugating verbs (though he actually gets it mostly right), and frustratedly asks what he needs French for anyhow. Bruce points out that if everyone knew each other's language, it might finally lead to world peace, an optimistic point of view, though one that would be put into action when Batman reconstituted the United World delegates with their minds in different bodies.

Overall, this is a great introduction to one of the show's best villains, and introducing several elements that would prove to be among the program's strong suits.

Keith R.A. DeCandido is a novelist, short fiction author, editor, martial artist, podcaster, amateur voice actor, and critic. In the latter capacity, he has been writing for the pop-culture site Tor.com since 2011, writing about *Star Trek*, *Stargate*, Marvel's Netflix TV series, *Doctor Who*, and lots more, including an extensive rewatch of *Batman '66* from 2015-2017. His other nonfiction on geeky things have appeared in magazines (*Entertainment Weekly, Star Trek Magazine, Library Journal, Publishers Weekly, Creem*) web sites (SciFi.com, Keith's own Patreon), and other anthologies (the *Outside In* series, BenBella's *Smart Pop* series, *Children of Time: The Companions of Doctor Who, A Long Time Ago: Exploring the Star Wars Cinematic Universe, Kobold's Guide to Comba*t, *New Worlds and New Civilizations: Exploring Star Trek Comics*, etc.) He also compiled the Tiny Book *Batman: Quotes from Gotham City* for Insight Editions.

On the fiction side, his first short story was in *The Ultimate Spider-Man* in 1994, and in the two-and-a-half decades since, he's written more than 50 novels, more than 100 short stories, and dozens of comics and graphic novels. His recent and upcoming work includes *Phoenix Precinct*, the sixth novel in his fantasy/police procedural series; *A Furnace Sealed*, the first book in a new urban fantasy series set in New York (with the sequel due out in 2020); *To Hell and Regroup*, a military SF novel in collaboration with David Sherman; the graphic novels *Icarus* and *Jellinek*; and short stories in the anthologies *Across the Universe, Bad Ass Moms, Brave New Girls: Adventures of Gals & Gizmos, Footprints in the Stars, Pangaea III, Unearthed, Thrilling Adventure Yarns*, and *Release the Virgins!* In 2009, he was given a Lifetime Achievement Award by the International Association of Media Tie-in Writers, which means he never needs to achieve anything ever again. Find out less at DeCandido.net.

ZOWIE!

The Caped Crusader vs. the Man of Bronze

"The Joker is Wild/Batman is Riled"

By Will Murray

I had never heard of the seminal pulp superhero Doc Savage when I first watched the third two-part episode of the *Batman* TV show back in January, 1966. So much of what fascinates me about "The Joker is Wild" and its sequel, "Batman is Riled" as an adult today actually went completely over my head back when I and my friends gathered around the family TV set. (We had the only color television in my neighborhood in those days, when *Batman* was a twice-weekly social event.)

"The Joker is Wild" opens with a bizarre scene more appropriate for a comic book than an episodic TV show. During a softball game in the Gotham State Penitentiary yard, the Joker contrives a fantastic escape before the eyes of the prison guards. The umpire—a Joker confederate—tosses him a trick ball. When the Joker hurls it toward the batter, the bat connects with explosive results. Amid an obscuring smoke screen, the Clown Prince of Crime is catapulted over the wall, literally "sprung" by a stupendous steel corkscrew spring that lifts the pitcher's mound aloft.

Never mind that the Grim Jester should have ended up a quadriplegic pile of broken limbs on the other side of the wall. He has escaped, landing on a strategically-placed net. Word reaches Commissioner Gordon that the Joker is loose. He puts in a call via the Bat Phone.

"The Joker?" frowns Bruce Wayne on the other end.

"Not him again!" exclaims Dick Grayson.

And off they race to their Bat-poles.

So faithfully did Producer Bill Dozier and his team replicate the tropes of a *Batman* comic book that they got away with this bald appropriation. If you read *Batman* in the early 60s, as I did, you were coming in the middle of a 25-year-old saga involving the Caped Crusader's ongoing battles with a revolving door of colorful supervillains, the most prominent of which was the Joker. Neither editor Jack Schiff nor replacement Julie Schwartz were big on recapping what had gone before. So when the Joker popped up in the pages of *Detective Comics* circa 1962, when I first encountered him, during the bizarre interlude in which Batman fought assorted aliens and giant monsters—that being the trend of the late 50s into the early 60s—his origin was not recounted for new readers. The Joker was simply back for another go-round with the Caped Crusader, kind of like Sonny Liston vs. Cassius Clay.

As a kid, I never questioned this convention. As an adult, rewatching "The Joker is Wild," I'm amazed they pulled it off so blithely. But they did. Nothing was set up for the viewer. That was the convention of the comics, so Dozier, director Bob Weis and his scripter (here, Dozier's son, Robert) replicated it faithfully. You were forever coming into the beginning of a story that was a continuation of an ongoing saga that had started long before you discovered the adventures of Batman and Robin.

Nor did the producers ever revisit the famous scene where Bruce

Wayne has a visitation from a flapping bat and his life's trajectory is forevermore altered. This wasn't laziness. It was what the Greek dramatists called *in media res*: "in the middle of things." The audience is dropped into an already unfolding story, skipping the often-boring character introductions, not to mention all narrative exposition. As a device, it was perfect for a half-hour TV show. The action had to grab audiences in the opening teaser sequence, lest viewers change channels.

I didn't know it at the time, but this episode was based on 1952 comic book story, "The Joker's Utility Belt." (*Batman* #73, October-November, 1952 and reprinted three months before this episode aired) The source story is not only a war of wits, but a battle of gadgets. Batman and his grinning foe continually yanked tricky devices out of their respective belts, flinging them with wild abandon. (Neither ever resorted to firearms; they were more resourceful than that.)

Before we explore the Doc Savage connection, a recap of the character's origin is in order. By that, I don't mean Batman's beginnings as a fictitious character, but the strip's genesis.

Bob Kane was a so-called "bigfoot" humor artist who had a friend named Bill Finger, an aspiring writer. Kane was working for the fledgling DC Comics, drawing assorted features when his editor asked him to dream up a superhero like Superman, who had recently debuted in that year of 1938.

Adventure strips were not Kane's forte. His initial idea was a red-and-black costumed character he provisionally called Bird-man. Summoning Finger to his home, Kane asked for help in developing the crude character.

Here accounts vary, if not contradict one another. But Finger appears to have pushed Bird-man in the direction of Bat-man. Both men were fans of a spooky 1930 mystery movie called *The Bat Whispers*. More importantly, both were readers of pulp magazines like *Doc Savage* and *The Shadow*, the leaders in the field as it existed in the late '30s.

Finger put it this way: "I was very much influenced by The Shadow and Doc Savage, The Phantom, things of that sort."

"He brought a lot of the early pulp writing style to Batman," observed Kane.

Finger further recalled, "We discussed Batman's potential. My idea was to have Batman be a combination of Douglas Fairbanks, Sherlock Holmes, The Shadow and Doc Savage as well."

The borrowing didn't cease with Batman's creators. When editor Mort Weisinger was lured away from pulp powerhouse Standard Magazines in 1940, he infused Batman with additional pulpy gimmicks. But let him tell it.

"I was the editor at *Phantom Detective,* which was a pulp magazine," Weisinger asserted. "And when I was the editor of *Batman*, when I originally came to DC, I was given Batman and Superman. I had to take care of Batman and Superman both. My idea of Batman was to give him some of the characteristics of the Phantom Detective. He had a special cave—the Bat Cave. But it was a lair where he did work. And he had a searchlight which the police commissioner turned on when he wanted Batman. I had created all these props for the Phantom Detective. So I took my little props and took my ballgame over to *Batman* and used them there. So in a way you can say there was a derivation from the pulps in the comics."

Weisinger is referring to the red signal light mounted atop the Clarion Building. Whenever newspaper publisher Frank Havens needed the Phantom, he lit the red navigation beacon that could be seen all over New York City. Hero Richard Curtis van Loan invariably spotted it and showed up, usually in disguise. This was the predecessor to the famed Bat Signal.

Van Loan's private laboratory in a Bronx tenement apartment was the precursor to the Bat Cave—although Kane pointed to the cave in *The Mark of Zorro,* where Zorro kept his steed, Tornado. (Both Batman and Zorro entered their respective underground lairs via a pivoting grandfather clock.) Weisinger was a huge Doc Savage fan, and knew author Lester Dent personally. The Bat Cave lab seems equally inspired by Doc's skyscraper laboratory.

Truth be told, Batman was built upon many preexisting foundations. Not until both creators were long dead and the franchise had mushroomed into global media phenomenon was it discovered that Batman's introductory story, "The Case of the Chemical Syndicate" was a direct steal from a 1936 Shadow novel by author Theodore Tinsley called *Partners of Peril.* It was loosely but consciously adapted in the same way "The Joker's Utility Belt" was reimagined as "The Joker is Wild."

Finger alone cannot be blamed for purloining Tinsley's plot. Kane was a notorious swipe artist, copying other artists wherever he could. One critical panel in "The Case of the Chemical Syndicate" showed Batman escaping a death trap in the form of a giant glass bell rapidly filling with lethal gas. Kane's illustration copied with modifications interior artist Tom Lovell's moody depiction of the same sequence, with Batman substituting for three trapped victims.

The Shadow was a two-gun cloaked mystery man who solved crimes through a mixture of scientific detection, escape artistry, and blazing .45 automatics. Like billionaire Bruce Wayne, he posed as an idle millionaire, Lamont Cranston. This was a popular pulp-magazine convention that had become a cliché by 1939. The Phantom Detective was another millionaire turned secret sleuth, as was the hero of *The Spider* magazine. Bruce Wayne was just another four-color iteration of that cliché.

Street & Smith's Doc Savage was cut from a different cloth. He was a scientist and adventurer. While wealthy, he was not a man-about-town type. Nor did Doc wear disguises, masks or cloaks.

As chronicled by his creator, Lester Dent, writing as Kenneth Robeson, Doc Savage employed scientific methods and frequently resorted to ingenious gadgets of his own creation.

Initially, Doc Savage carried his gadgets in a special many-pocketed leather vest, but by 1937 he had switched to a utility belt similar to the cartridge belts U.S. soldiers wore. Instead of being constructed of khaki-colored canvas, and stuffed with bullets, Doc's "kit" was yellow and the pockets crammed with various gadgets. They ran the gamut from small gas pellets and smoke bombs to a folding grappling hook handy for climbing walls, and even more elaborate devices.

After Batman got going, he began pulling similar stuff out of his utility belt, which not coincidentally was also canary-yellow. The chief difference was that instead of snap-pockets, Batman's belt was studded with cylindrical containers. His black Batarang—evidently modeled after a yellow boomerang The Shadow carried for casting rope lines to building cornices for climbing purposes—was also carried therein.

Kane and Finger lifted everything in sight. Their genius was to make it work. Nor is this an indictment of their creative abilities. Lester Dent often said his Doc Savage was a mixture of Sherlock Holmes, Tarzan and other characters. The Shadow was a version of Sherlock Holmes wearing Dracula's cape and possessing the escape knowledge of the great Harry Houdini. All great characters seem to be built on those that came before them. Batman is no exception.

Kane also pointed to these diverse characters as inspirations. "The first year of Batman, he was a vigilante and we were influenced by horror films and emulated a Dracula look. I loved mystery movies and serials; the Shadow on radio was also a big influence."

Even the Joker wasn't entirely original. Both Kane and Finger cited the grotesque silent film character of Gwynplaine, from *The Man Who Laughs*, as their inspiration. The Joker's gruesome origin—his features were bleached and disfigured by acid--was no doubt too gruesome for TV—not that Dozier ever considered wasting footage on origins. (But it was implied by the convict Joker's stark white face—hinting that his pallor was not of theatrical make-up.)

The clown-as-criminal motif came from other sources. Zorro's creator, Johnston McCulley, wrote a famous series of pulp stories about a cracked Robin Hood calling himself the Crimson Clown. But he was a good guy. The Phantom battled an evil Crimson Clown in 1934, as well as challenging foes such as the Keyboard Killer, who taunted the law with song-lyric clues to future crimes, an M. O. Finger copied for the Joker.

"We were talking about getting a supervillain who would play perennial, but deathly, jokes on the Batman—jokes that were killing, and not just comedy pranks," remembered Kane.

One of Theodore Tinsley's short stories, "The Grim Joker," spotlighted a white-faced master criminal who went by that name. The story was published in the back pages of *The Whisperer*, a mystery man who was in reality Commissioner James Gordon. He debuted in 1936. It's hard to imagine that Gotham City's police commissioner was not named in his honor.

As Kane once said of his collaborator, "He was a pulp reader. As a matter of fact, I read all the pulps that Bill Finger read. He'd give me his magazines and I did read them. I was influenced by Doc Savage and the pulps, to some extent."

The casting of Cesar Romero as the Joker accomplished the seemingly impossible, transforming a bizarre caricature of a harlequin into a TV-palatable prancing comedian whose homicidal tendencies, while fully on display, were never frightening.

"I also wanted my style a little cartoony—a cross between Dick Tracy and illustration," noted Kane. "That's why the Penguin and the Joker are still kind of cartoony. I drew the Joker straighter and more illustratively than my ghost artists. They made him grotesquely clown-like, longer and thinner, and so exaggerated he looks like a buffoon."

The six foot, three, 59-year-old Romero straddled the difference between Kane and his ghost artists. The fact that Dozier's initial acting choice declined the part was undoubtedly for the best.

As Dozier observed, "Jose Ferrer was my first choice for the Joker. He either didn't want to do it or couldn't. He has kicked himself ever since. 'Butch' Romero, whom I had known forever, was the second choice for the Joker, and I am not sure he did not turn out better than Jose. I am not sure that Jose would have captured the frivolity and the ludicrousness of the character."

Ferrer had played Cyrano de Bergerac on Broadway and in a 1964 French film—an outsized role which may have suggested the Joker to Dozier. But Romero made the part his own.

"When I get into an outfit like that," the seasoned actor once said, "I'm not going to go 'Oh ha ha', I'm going to go 'Ooh ha ha ha ha'...you fall right into it. I thoroughly enjoyed playing the Joker."

I mentioned that "The Case of the Chemical Syndicate" was loosely adapted from *Partners of Peril.* In this case, it was compressed to its essential story beats. When Robert Dozier adapted "The Joker's Utility Belt" for television, he necessarily expanded it significantly in order to convert a 12-page sequential story into two half-hour TV episodes. For example, the opening prison-escape sequence did not appear in the source comic book story—although it might have been lifted from another Joker story.

Rewatching the episode after several decades, I was shocked by how much Adam West's Batman mirrored classic Doc Savage. A straight arrow, dedicated unswervingly to battling crime and criminals the police could not outwit, the two crimefighters might have been cousins. But that was the *modus operandi* of many self-appointed extra-legal vigilantes of their original era. Batman's stilted, overly formal manner of speech, elevated morality and Boy Scout attitudes are distilled from Doc Savage, but exaggerated in the campy way of the show.

The Doc Savage influence permeated everything, including the corny Vaudevillian humor, a Lester Dent specialty. Doc was a scientific detective and kept himself in top shape through rigorous exercise. So did Batman. Revisiting Adam West's Caped Crusader, I now saw him as Doc Savage dressed as a batty version of The Shadow. It was a revelation.

I was floored when, while attempting to enter the closed Gotham Museum because he suspects the Joker is concealed within, Batman pulls a bat-drill from his utility belt and breaks in. Audiences of that era would have seen this as a nod to James Bond, but I recognized an earlier influence. Doc Savage. After Batman is knocked out and the Joker's "comic cohorts in crime" are carrying him out, the Caped Crusader slyly opens one eye, slips a device out of a belt pouch and drops it to the floor.

The gimmick resembles two linked balls of different substances. Upon impact with the floor, they shatter and the chemicals presumably combine, producing a purple gas coincidently the same outlandish hue as the Joker's coat. "Bat gas!" he exclaims, retreating from the spreading cloud. But I recognized Doc's most potent non-lethal weapon: Glass bombs which release anesthetic gas when broken.

His hirelings overcome, the Joker slips down a handy trapdoor that has no business being in a museum. How very Comic Book.

"That cursed utility belt again!" rages the Clown Prince of Crime. "I swear by all that is holy I will never be fooled by that insidious unconstitutional device again!"

Fuming at being defeated again, the Joker repairs to his lair and decides that he must devise a utility belt of his own. Which he does. But his belt—identical to Batman's except for the Joker-face buckle—is brimming with novelties and other tricks suitable for committing crazy conspiratorial crimes.

Here, as the battle of utility belts commences, the storyline tracks closely with the inspirational comic book. Following a clue, Batman deduces that the Joker will appear at a performance of *Pagliacci*. Which he does—disguised as the famous clown! During that mad clash Batman is overcome by sneezing powder and captured. His unmasking on live television becomes the episode's cliffhanger.

"Batman is Riled" opens with the Caped Crusader plucking a miniature Bat-missile from his belt, using it to set off the sprinkler system. The Joker counters this with a smoke pellet, thereby making his escape in the resultant confusion once more.

The action-rituals of captures and escapes were a tried-and-true Doc Savage convention—although it hardly originated with the Man of Bronze. Batman's creators milked it to death. If you watched *The Man from U.N.C.L.E.* (yet another Doc Savage-inspired series), this was familiar stuff.

A fresh merry-go-round of circular action finds Batman and Robin thwarted when the Joker implausibly swaps utility belts in mid-melee and an unwitting Batman throws a gimmick at this fiendish foe, only to become entangled in noisy fireworks and Fourth-of-July streamers. The laughing Joker flees his reach again.

"That tricky devil," fumes Batman. "He's hit us below the belt!"

It all culminates in a scheme so audacious that it might have been torn from a Doc Savage adventure. To please his moll, Queenie (Nancy Kovack), the Joker decides to hijack the luxury liner *S. S Gotham* upon its launch. Batman is selected to christen it. Following the comic book plot, the Joker replaces the champagne cork with one he carries in his belt. When Batman shatters the bottle, knockout gas is released. Events move so swiftly that this fourth capture is not tiresome, but simply another wrinkle in the unending carousel of mayhem that is their working relationship.

Facing execution on live TV, Batman turns the tables for the final time with still another ingenious gimmick palmed from yet another pocket of his inexhaustible utility belt.

Seriously, it is all quintessentially Doc Savage. Even the Joker's belt contents. For Doc was not above mixing sneezing and itching powder and other tricky novelties with his usual arsenal of smoke bombs, anesthetic gas pellets and the Thermite fuses (another handy substance Bill Finger borrowed from the Man of Bronze).

Next to the opening Riddler episodes, the Joker's introduction is my favorite *Batman* sequence. The balance between straight action and campy comedy was still in equipoise. Sure, the dialogue was pure Comic Book, but it was identical to the dialogue Bill Finger was writing for *Detective Comics* in those days. In the era before Stan Lee-style writing took hold, that was how you did it!

As I recall, I watched *Batman* well into season one before it dawned on me that the showrunners were spoofing comic book conventions. You can forgive me for being slow on the uptake, I think, since the first three Batman villains were the Riddler, the Penguin and the Joker. Between their giggling and cackling and quacking, the hilarity seemed all on the villains' side. I wasn't reading Adam West's deadpan delivery as sly humor. I wanted my superheroes straight. And for a time, that's what I thought I was watching. Silly me.

Cesar Romero's first turn as the Joker had him laughing uproariously from start to finish. His flamboyant portrayal no doubt contributed to, if not cemented, the branding of *Batman* as "camp." For TV, it worked. Sadly, the dramatic element soon succumbed to loud cries for more camp, and the willingness of guest-villains such as Romero to lay it on with a Bat-trowel.

"You know, what we did was a hoot and a howl," he once observed.

How closely are Batman and Doc Savage linked?

Consider this: in the late 60s, after *Batman* had run its course on TV, Bill Dozier teamed with ex-*Rifleman* Chuck Connors to film the first of what was planned to be a series of Doc Savage movies. Issues with the rights caused the project to collapse, but had Doc Savage gone forward, Producer Dozier would have stood on firm and familiar ground. I wouldn't have been surprised if the Man of Bronze had worn his custom-made yellow utility belt and detonated gas pellets in a way that would have brought Doc fans Bob Kane and Bill Finger to their feet, applauding wildly.

And when producer George Pal successfully cleared the rights, his 1975 film, *Doc Savage, Man of Bronze,* was widely derided as "high camp" in the mold of—you guessed it, Bill Dozier's *Batman*...

Will Murray discovered Batman early in 1962 during the infamous Jack Schiff era. He contributed three Batman short stories to the Further Adventures series of Bantam Books Batman anthologies, "Bone," "The City That Could Not Breathe" and "Seize the Night." Famed as the creator of a completely different superheroic rodent, the Unbeatable Squirrel Girl, Murray is also the author of over 70 books and novels, including the Wild Adventures series, which revived Doc Savage, The Shadow, The Spider, Tarzan of the Apes and King Kong. Check out www.adventuresinbronze.com.

ZOK!

Art, Nonsense, and Money

"Instant Freeze/Rats Like Cheese"
By Pat Evans

"Somewhere in between the inauspicious, comic book beginnings of the one-off Batman villain Mr. Zero in 1959 and the deeply tragic character of the 1992 Animated Series lies Mr. Freeze, 1966.

But beware, for even in this very specific universe there are several different versions of this dastardly criminal."

Of course our unseen narrator here is referring to the three different actors who portrayed Mr. Freeze in his three series appearances.

Sadly it's his very first on-screen appearance—in the form of the great veteran actor George Sanders—that is the least remembered.

The other two that followed him, film director Otto Preminger and Eli Wallach (who both took the role at the behest of their grandchildren) are more widely remembered than Sanders by a long stretch.

Evidence of this can easily be found in the most recent waves of licensed merchandise for the 1966 series. Three Mr. Freeze figures, a mini bust and a Funko pop were released. Of those, all were based on the Otto Preminger version except for one figure of Eli Wallach that was released as a limited variant.

No George Sanders version.

Luckily I have made a few very intelligent observations about why that might be, along with incredibly sharp analyses of the character and the episodes. And now, humbly, I present them to you.

Writer Max Hodge plucked the character out of obscurity from the aforementioned comic book, *Batman* #121. In this one-and-done story, a scientist accidentally spills freezing compound on himself while developing a "cold gun" weapon. He then puts on a goofy union suit, (red and green, for no readily discernable reason. Christmas colors maybe?) along with a clear, rounded glass helmet and commits some minor ice-related heists with his freeze/laser gun. Then Batman and Robin catch him and throw him into a steam bath, instantly curing him. The End.

So, right off the bat credit has to go to Max for seeing past the limited scope of the character as drawn in the comic and breathing new life into him for the show. We can also be glad that production changed his costume from the comic book as it does look quite pedestrian. The overall design is not bad but the color scheme was a disaster. Honestly, Google it.

Important Point #1: *Costuming can go a long way if you're a super-villain.*

The series also gifted him with a slightly more interesting backstory: Instead of clumsily spilling freezing chemicals on himself, they wisely made Batman responsible for his frozen condition, accidentally causing the "Instant Freeze" compound to spill on him during a fight in his laboratory.

Thus his simple dual motivations are established: revenge against

Batman and funding his expensive sub-zero environment through robbery. Nonetheless Batman feels a responsibility to rehabilitate "the poor devil", as is his wont.

Sanders' version reads more like a Bond villain, lounging about in lovely tailored suits (and the most glorious gold smoking jacket I've ever seen) whereas his successors appeared only in the full-on Freeze costume. His "super air-conditioned" mountain lair was jettisoned in subsequent outings as well in favor of flashier, arctic-themed digs.

Which leads to the other key difference between Sanders and his successors: scenery-chewing. Since Batman and the other upright citizens of Gotham are so literally straight and narrow, that's how they are played in general: seriously. The villains are meant to be an outrageous counterpoint to this. Thus a certain amount of scenery-chewing was virtually guaranteed, likely encouraged and what's more it worked in the show's favor. Sanders doesn't chew the scenery as Freeze, nor does he underplay it. I think he strikes a pretty good balance between calculating and maniacal.

Anyway, I've heard that the intent was to bring Sanders back for the next second season episodes (also written by Max Hodge) but he was unavailable due to other filming commitments. I don't think he was hated by audiences or by the production (unlike Otto Preminger, who was so disliked by the crew that he was deliberately replaced). It would have been very interesting to have him back in the role and I wonder how much would have changed, approach-wise, had he returned. Would he have eventually gotten his own submarine lair and pet seal? The mind reels.

Whatever the reasons for the changes the result is that the more flamboyant Otto Preminger and Eli Wallach performances are generally remembered more fondly over George Sanders'. Which is a shame, because he's every bit as good as they are, just more understated. I will grant you the upgraded look was more memorable and fun overall, but still, that smoking jacket...

Not that I think his costume is *bad* per se, it just doesn't stand out in the way the costumes of some of the more memorable villains do, and I think it goes a long way (along with the more cartoonish performances) to explain why the other two Freezes are better remembered, in particular Preminger with his big blue bald head and bushy eyebrows. Perhaps the producers were simply trying to bring Freeze in line with the other super-criminals on the show, who were never out of costume save for sporting prison garb or wearing a disguise to fool the authorities (King Tut, with his dual personality, could be considered an exception).

Now let's talk helmets. Unfortunately Sander's helmet looks a bit like a leftover from a low budget 50's sci-fi movie. This is one area in which Mr. Zero's look, with his clear, round glass helmet, was arguably superior.

Quick Mr. Freeze Helmet Fun Fact: *the clear glass helmet was re-instated as part of Mr. Freeze's garb on the first animated version of the character, Filmation's "Batman/Superman Hour" in 1968. The next time Freeze appeared in animated form on "Batman: The Animated Series" in 1992, a modified domed version was used.*

Not only was the helmet kind of *blah* visually, the actor's voice was obviously not able to be recorded clearly through it either; every line while he is wearing it has been overdubbed after the fact. My suspicion is that this was a prime motivation for the production team dumping it in favor of the "freeze collar" design. Using the on set audio is almost always preferable to ADR, or Automatic Dialogue Replacement, which basically means your actors come in and re-dub their lines in a studio.

Speaking of dialogue, Sander's version lobbed a few low-key ice-related remarks ("Zat is ze vay ze ice cube crumbles") at the Caped Crusaders and had a corny fondness for Baked Alaska. Still, nowhere near the magnitude of the 1997 big-screen Joel Schumacher version, which crammed ice puns into the script as if human lives depended on it and delivered them with the subtlety and grace of, well, an Austrian bodybuilder with a comically impenetrable accent. I find this extremely amusing as, although it would have been acceptable in terms of the tone of the show, the *Batman* writers knew enough to steer clear of such low-hanging fruit. Akiva Goldsman, the writer of *Batman and Robin*, most certainly knew better and did it anyway, with a level of zealotry that would shame a kamikaze pilot.

There is a point to mentioning the Arnie version beyond poking fun at it, entertaining as that may be. But first I (and really all '66 Bat-fans) must thank the great Wally Wingert for once again preventing some important bits of the show's history from permanently fading into the ether.

After writer Max Hodge passed away in 2007, Wally had the foresight to attend his estate sale here in Los Angeles to see what, if any, Batman related goodies he might find. And boy did he find a doozy, particularly in regards to our discussion here.

It seems Max had a good look around at all the hype surrounding the 1997 film (not hard, as it was ubiquitous) and saw all the Mr. Freeze merchandise which prompted the question foremost in every writer's mind: "Where's my money?"

To that end, he created a 17-page document that asked just that question of Warner Brothers.

Ten years later, Wally walked out of his estate sale with it.

The document is fascinating to read—it's less a legal document than a guy stating his case to the powers that be and saying "Hey, what gives?" In fact, the document is charmingly addressed in just that way: "To the Powers That Be".

He makes a good case too, noting he changed the name from "Zero", which he felt was too negative, to "Freeze" and introduced the character's Teutonic origins and accent, which was certainly continued in the form of Schwarzenegger.

Another connection that Max did not make but that I noticed between his and the Schwarzenegger version: their obsession with diamonds!

Max also kept a daily diary and the document includes photocopied pages from 1965-66 regarding his progress with his *Batman* writing assignment. It is a real treat to see these.

What finally became of all this—whether he was ignored by Warner Brothers or they silently slid him a check to appease him—is unknown.

In my view Max should absolutely be given shared credit for the creation of Mr. Freeze. Certainly he based it off of Mr. Zero, but without his refinements the character might have remained as flat as his comic counterpart. Without him there likely would have been no award-winning animated version and no ginormous check for Arnold.

Since Bob Kane, Dave Wood and Sheldon "Shelly" Moldoff are credited with creating the original Mr. Zero character, I would like to advance the notion that the following credit- or something like it- be applied to any future Mr. Freeze projects:

Mr. Freeze created by Max Hodge with Bob Kane, Dave Wood and Sheldon Moldoff

Seems fair to me.

Now I suppose at some point I must get around to discussing the actual episodes in question, and now seems a good a time as any. Instead of a blow-by-blow analysis, I'd like to pick a few key scenes and moments that I think really detail the genius of all involved. As it happens the first of these is actually the very beginning, so that's where we'll start.

The episode opens cold (Note: NOT an ice pun) with a good quality bit of stock footage of happy skaters at an indoor ice rink, skating along with some happy skating music. This reverie is suddenly shattered as we cut to the exterior of the rink, while the score quickly dips into danger music and the sounds of a woman screaming are heard off screen, presumably from inside the rink.

The rink doors burst open to reveal a mysterious figure in a silver spacesuit-like outfit and helmet carrying some sort of futuristic looking gun, along with three guys wearing silly light blue ski sweaters and hats. They quickly pile into the back of a waiting ice cream truck idling on the curb and peel out as panicked patrons begin pouring out of the venue, still in their ice skates no less.

One of the female skaters flags down a Gotham motorcycle cop and excitedly tells him what has happened, that a kooky-looking guy melted the rink with a big flamethrower (for reasons that are never really explained, now that I think of it.) The cop tears off in (again, not a pun) hot pursuit.

By the way, if the female patron looks familiar, that's because it's none other than a young Teri Garr in one of her early TV appearances. Teri would again appear in the Batman universe some thirty years later as the mother of Terry McGinnis, Bruce Wayne's protégé and heir to the mantle of Batman in the animated series *Batman Beyond.* The series was developed by Bruce Timm and Paul Dini, who breathed new life in to the Mr. Freeze character in *Batman: The Animated Series* a few years previously. It's all a rich tapestry, folks.

The chase through the streets of Gotham is awesome, with the truck making some truly boss cornering moves. Here I'd like to give credit to Troy Melton who plays Freeze's henchman "Chill" and performs the fantastic driving in the scene. Troy was a seasoned veteran and one of the founding members of the Stuntmen's Association of Motion Pictures. He makes it look easy.

As the truck wildly careens around the streets, the back bursts open to reveal our as yet unidentified villain, with his aforementioned heat gun. But instead of flames, out shoots a wicked blast of some sort of white powdery substance that he aims at the road.

It soon becomes clear that this is some sort of cold gun as well, as the road becomes slick with ice, causing the motorcycle cop to lose control of his bike.

This brings us to the second driving stunt. In a continuous overhead crane shot, the cop lays down the bike, skids to a stop mid-frame, rolls over and sits up groggily. It's very impressive!

A quick aside: Being a prop guy, I absolutely love the Freeze gun (a re-purposed *Lost in Space* rifle in fact. The prop makers from LIS also handled many of the *Batman* props). It's a functioning device that shoots a convincingly powerful burst of air from the twin canisters strapped to his back and, later, a cool animated laser heat beam as well, another element brought forward from the Mr. Zero character.

I'm not sure exactly what the canisters on Freeze's back are, but they look very much like fire extinguishers. Bright red fire extinguishers.

My point being the first thing you think when you see the evil villain's big weapon is "Fire extinguishers". I always wondered why they didn't just spray paint those suckers blue or silver? I would say maybe they ran out of time or money, but spray paint is fast and cheap and the same red tanks were used in Otto Preminger's version. Since, as discussed, his costume received several snazzy upgrades it remains a puzzle why they left his damn freeze canisters *bright red.* Even Mr. Zero, with his pitiable sense of color, sported a blue tank on his back!

Love the gun, hate the tanks!

They did finally rectify this for the Eli Wallach episodes by simply hiding the tanks off screen while he fired the gun. I have to be honest here: as I'm typing this I find myself asking, "How the hell do I know all this?" followed closely by "Why the hell do I know all this?' and finally "Why the hell am I telling you all this?"

Moving on, the next standout for me is the first scene at Wayne Manor. Everyone is on top of their game here. Burt Ward shines with his golly-gee admiration of Gotham's baseball hero Paul Diamante and Madge Blake has a couple of nice little Aunt Harriet moments. But where the scene really impresses is the intricate yet subtle choreography once Alfred delivers a trademark coded message to Bruce that Commissioner Gordon is on the line for Batman.

The camera glides subtly forward through the hallway with the departing luncheon company, Bruce making friendly small talk with his guests and simultaneously exchanging intense knowing glances signaling Dick and Alfred while deftly making an exit into the study to answer the hotline. Alfred is finally left alone in the foyer with Aunt Harriet where he calmly assuages her concerns about Bruce and Dick's activities, as ever. It's a graceful and clever ballet conducted by director Robert Butler and flawlessly executed by the cast.

The next great moment for me is a simple static shot, but no less elegant. After hopping out of the "Portable Freezing Chamber" in the Batcave, Batman stands shivering in frame, with Alfred and Robin flanking him. He accepts hot tea from Alfred, whilst explaining their preventive measures against Mr. Freeze and daintily drinking his tea, Bat-gloves and all. The shot holds for over a minute and a half! Also note how Adam subtly reduces his shivering and recovers his strength over the duration of the scene. For me, this scene shows just how thoroughly he owned the character of Batman.

Personally I feel enough cannot be said about Robert Butler's direction in these episodes. The man knew when to move the camera, and when NOT to move it. His instincts were phenomenal in my opinion.

A few smaller moments I love:

- There's one very quick but wonderful shot in the Batcave shortly after the Freezing Chamber scene- a short, quick pan that starts on the phone and follows Adam as he does a neat little spin and deftly answers the call with a "Yes, Commissioner." It's a small flourish but another excellent example of Robert Butler's smart direction and instincts.
- Batman and Robin stunt doubles Hubie Kerns and Victor Paul do a marvelous parkour up the front façade of a hotel. Often it's obvious when they have switched from Burt and Adam to Hubie and Victor, but this blends perfectly with the previous footage of Adam and Burt arriving in the Batmobile (and Burt cheekily walking across the top of the car). Hubie and Victor make it look absolutely effortless.
- The Dynamic Duo makes excellent use of one of the coolest, unsung Batcave props: The Giant Lighted Lucite Map of Gotham City.

I would also be remiss if I didn't mention the glowing freeze effect used when Freeze uses his cold gun on Batman and Robin. It is gloriously low-tech and I absolutely love it. Mr. Freeze's hot and cold zones are fun too; in fact Adam praised FX man L.B. Abbot's work on these episodes in his 1994 *Back to the Batcave* memoir.

If there's one place the episode falls down, it's the first fight scene, which is tantalizingly teased as a battle between the five fake Mr. Freezes and five fake Batmen that Freeze has hired to confuse the citizenry, constabulary and Caped Crusaders as he executes his dastardly plan.

This premise had a lot of promise. Robin could have been confused as to which is the real Batman ("It's me Robin, don't you recognize me?" "No, Boy Wonder, *I'm* the real Batman"). We do get one hastily delivered line to this effect, but it doesn't really land. You could have had fun visuals like Batman bopping the heads of two Mr. Freezes together ("Bonk!"). Alas, it's just a big, sloppy free-for-all, with the occasional Freeze gun shooting off here and there. Pretty disappointing.

One more thing that always cracks me up: watch the fake Batman second from the right when they enter the room. Most of the Batmen look pretty great but this guy has absolutely *no chin*. The bottom of the mask hangs off his face in a comically droopy fashion.

But overall this is a standout arc for me, and definitely worth your time to watch. The whole cast is terrific, the script is solid fun and, as mentioned before, George Sanders handles the Mr. Freeze role capably. Again I think with the signature costume he would have certainly been remembered more widely in the role.

And as a parting shot Adam delivers one of the finest lines of dry dialogue in the entire series after surviving Mr. Freeze's final frozen deathtrap:

"Naturally you didn't know I was wearing my special Super-Thermo-B long underwear... for extreme cold!"

It's easy to see why Adam cited these Mr. Freeze episodes as two of his all-time favorites, along with the pilot episode. I personally do not feel it is coincidence that both of these entries were directed by Robert Butler.

One more thing of note to mention: "Instant Freeze" contains the second of the only true deaths in the series. The first occurred in the second episode "Hot off the Griddle", when Molly falls into the Atomic Pile. In this case a butler is frozen by Freeze's cold gun and we see him start to fall over. It quickly cuts away and we hear a shattering noise as a poor secretary faints, presumably from seeing the poor fellow breaking into a million pieces, while Freeze's goons madly cackle.

I'll finish with one more very obscure bit of trivia for the most diehard of diehards out there. This again, as so many things do, involves the inimitable Wally Wingert.

Now, Wally and I occasionally commiserate on some of the more obtuse points of the show, identifying props and costumes, things like that. And with the clarity of the Blu-ray releases, new details reveal themselves and plunge us further down the rabbit hole of these types of discussions.

You will notice in the very first Wayne Manor scenes in "Instant Freeze" Bruce is wearing a club jacket with a snazzy patch on the breast. This is meant to be the Wayne Family crest. Adam recounted in one of his autobiographies that the motto on the crest was Latin for "Art, Nonsense, and Money". Gotta love that.

So in preparing for a huge 1966 Batman exhibit at the Hollywood Museum spearheaded by Wally, the subject of the patch arose as we were planning on dressing mannequins as Bruce Wayne and Dick Grayson in some of their signature civilian apparel. Wally was rightly insistent on having the club coat with the patch for Adam's outfit.

Easier said than done.

We both went and looked at every frame we could find of Adam in the jacket and despite our best efforts couldn't make out what was on it, exactly. The key came when Wally noticed the very top of the patch appeared to be a crown! A-ha! It's based on something British—this made perfect sense to us as Jan Kemp, the show's costume designer, was from England.

Okay, so he based it on some royal patch design, but what? Being as my dad was a Naval flight officer and I was an Airman in the Navy myself, it suddenly dawned on me: it's probably some kind of Royal Air Force or Navy patch. A-ha again!

After image searching I was finally able to match up the scant visual details with a Royal Air Force Ordnance Division patch. It was a dead ringer. We had definitely found the exact design. It even had the banners with a Latin motto on it!

We also had to decide how exactly to translate the phrase in Latin; there seemed to be a couple options and we had no other reference point other than Adam's quote. You certainly couldn't make it out on screen. In the end I think we just made a best guess.

From there we tried to figure out how to have our own patch made and realized it was actually quite a specialized thing (made with metal wire!) and the only suitable manufacturer was in England. What's more, they only made high-quality versions of the official military patch; they would be unable to put our custom Latin phrase on it.

About this time we started thinking more carefully about things. Knowing the frantic pace and workload of the show, would they have gone through the time, trouble and expense of actually making a special patch with a secret gag phrase written in Latin that would likely never be fully readable on camera? Or was it more likely that Jan Kemp had one of his family member's military patches in a drawer, pulled it out and said, "This'll do".

That was when we realized we'd been had. Adam, the well-known jokester, had pulled one over on us, decades after the fact and from the Great Beyond no less. Now *that's* some next-level pranking.

Wally was good friends with Adam for over thirty years and so shared quite a few special moments with him over that time. I only met Adam briefly on three occasions, but I fully count this as a fourth encounter. Posthumous as it was, it was definitely a special Adam moment for me.

Art, Nonsense, and Money indeed, old chum.

Special thanks to Wally Wingert and Troy Maynus for their invaluable assistance.

Pat Evans is a lifelong fan and a historian of Batman, and has a particular fondness for the TV series starring his childhood hero Adam West. Pat was an integral part of the first-ever 1966 Batman exhibit at the Hollywood Museum, donating many pieces from his own collection and creating several replica props for display.

ZLONK!

The Legend of Zelda

"Zelda the Great/A Death Worse Than Fate"
By Steven Thompson

Ladies aaaaaand gentlemen! May I have your attention please? Today, right here on these very pages, you are going to meet the world's greatest escape artist, the world's most renowned prestidigitator, that magnificent mistress of misbegotten misdirection and magic, the one, the only...ZELDA THE GREAT!

Holy Houdini, Batman! What's so "Great" about Zelda the Great?

This one-hit wonder Special Guest Villainess is generally considered a bit of an also-ran amongst Bat-fans, a barely remembered trivia question who simply couldn't hold her own beside such classic rogues' gallery residents as the Joker, Catwoman, the Mad Hatter, or even that crazy cowboy, Shame. Why, even the actress who played Zelda abandoned her for a different guest villainess down the line—Olga! Queen of the Bessarovian Cossacks!

That was Oscar winner Anne Baxter, Best Supporting Actress in 1947 for *The Razor's Edge* and Best Actress nominee in 1951 for *All About Eve*.

Legend has long had it that all the big stars wanted to play Bat-villains but, if you look, there really weren't that many. Recognizable faces like Burgess Meredith, Cesar Romero, and David Wayne were never really A-list stars, but Anne Baxter certainly was.

Only seventeen when she made her Hollywood debut in 1940, Anne was quickly signed to a seven-year contract with 20th Century Fox. Working her way up from small roles in major releases such as *Five Graves to Cairo* and Orson Welles' *The Magnificent Ambersons*, her Oscar followed, just six years into her film career. The 1950s started with Baxter in her signature title role in *All About Eve* and saw her also working with Alfred Hitchcock in *I Confess* and Cecil B. DeMille on *The Ten Commandments*.

By late in the decade, television beckoned and a whole new career on the small screen followed. In real life, Baxter married an Australian rancher and spent much of her time Down Under, but the life of a housewife wasn't for her. After a brief slowdown in her acting, she moved back into movies and television, with *Batman* being one of her first TV jobs upon her return.

Himself an Academy Award Nominee (for *The Apartment*, 1960), Canadian actor Jack Kruschen chews the scenery as the heavily accented Eivol Eckdol. Although a familiar face in television and films from the 1950s on, it was radio where the multi-talented Kruschen had really thrived in character parts. Kruschen's voice and its many accents could be heard on scores of network series including *Nightbeat*, *Dragnet*, *Gunsmoke*, and *Suspense*. He also acted in recurring roles on *Pete Kelly's Blues* and *Broadway is my Beat*.

On the big screen, Kruschen worked opposite everyone from John Wayne and Abbott and Costello to Elvis Presley and Chevy Chase before his death in 2002.

The *Batman* series quickly developed a reputation of using seasoned actors. Neil Hamilton—Commissioner Gordon—had been a leading man in late silent and early talkies. Alfred—Alan Napier—

had once played Sherlock Holmes. Frankie Darro played a newsman in "Zelda the Great" and also toplined a series of comedies opposite Mantan Moreland, and the doctor in this episode was character actor Douglas Dumbrille, whose credits went back to 1913, here in his final acting role.

Even the Zelda director was an old-time star. Norman Foster had been a Paramount contract lead in the early 1930s and later alternated acting with directing. Although long gone, he actually had a new credit in 2018 when he co-starred in a major role in the decades-delayed Orson Welles film, *The Other Side of the Wind.*

"Zelda the Great" is an easy episode (in two parts, naturally) to make fun of and yet it's actually one of the most entertaining entries, partially because it doesn't fit the show's usual formula. You know: Batman is called, the Dynamic Duo pull up to the front of Police Headquarters, Commissioner Gordon tells them about a criminal and they give chase, inevitably ending up in a fist fight with colorful sound effect words popping up in mid-air and a cliffhanger death-trap that our heroes can't possibly escape waiting at the end of Part One! I mean, come on. Except for specific details, that describes pretty much every Batman episode of the first two seasons.

Except Zelda's.

For one, there's no fist fight at all. In either part! Zelda, the first of numerous female villains on the series, simply doesn't have any minions to send into battle. Not even magician's assistants, apparently. Batman and Robin never even get captured in Part One, so no death trap for them. And in the end, Zelda turns out to not even be so bad after all. It was her associate, that "mad Albanian genius," Eivol Eckdol, who's both avaricious and out to kill the Caped Crusaders.

This particular episode is also one of only a relative few to have been directly adapted from a Batman comic book story. In this case, writer Lorenzo Semple, Jr., then living in Spain, apparently picked up the then-current U.S. issue of *Detective Comics* (#346, cover dated December 1965, but on the stands in October) and just sat down at his typewriter to adapt John Broome's story, "Batman's Inescapable Doom-Trap."

The four-color version of the story is pretty close to what ended up on television, but with a few medium-sized differences and one decidedly major change. It seems that in the transition between the two mediums, the antagonist had a sex-change.

It all began when Producer William Dozier sent a memo to Semple, who had developed the series and served as its Executive Story Editor, regarding the need for more villains of the opposite sex. Other than Catwoman—a long-abandoned comic book character who had premiered in the 1940s but who, at that point, hadn't appeared in a new story in more than a decade—there simply weren't any memorable female adversaries for the Dynamic Duo. In the comics, Poison Ivy was created around that same time to remedy that very problem and presumably to appear on the series. For some reason, she never did.

Semple's original script for what was intended to be the third episode (after the expensive Riddler pilot and the first Penguin appearance) had used the bearded male villain of the comic book, Carnado, a rather slimy stage magician. The writer certainly couldn't change the sex of well-known enemies like the Joker or the Penguin and, of course, "Mrs." Freeze just wouldn't have been the same. But Carnado? He had never appeared anywhere before and, plot wise, there was no reason at all why *he* couldn't be...she. Thus was born Zelda.

Semple, after a particularly impressive career that included writing the screenplays for *Three Days of the Condor*, *Never Say Never Again*, *Flash Gordon*, and *Papillon*, stated flat out in his *Emmy TV Legends* interview, "I still consider *Batman* the best thing I ever wrote."

The uniqueness of the two parts of "Zelda the Great" may well make *it* the best Batman episode he ever wrote!

Throughout the adventure, we're presented with mixed signals regarding Zelda herself. "All I ever wanted to be was a poor but honest magician," she says. A two-story sign on the side of a building in downtown Gotham City refers to Zelda the Great as "the World's Foremost Illusionist and Escape Artiste," and "Even Greater than Houdini!" We know that for at least three years, she's been appearing onstage in increasingly daring escapes in Gotham.

And yet Robin notes that he and Bruce had gone to see her act on his last birthday and even gone backstage to meet her. So how come when they see her at the jewelry store, neither one recognizes her as a world-famous magician, apparently widely advertised at that very moment, whom they'd recently met socially, and who was one of only twenty-seven female magicians licensed to practice in Gotham?

Beyond that one annoying flaw, though, it is, as noted, an enjoyable, atypical episode in which this poor woman is forced into a life of crime. Well, not so much a life, really. More like one day a year. In order to continually improve her escape act, Zelda purchases fresh, complex, dangerous, and death-defying traps annually for $100,000 from Eckdol. Apparently, her presumed gigs and personal appearances on TV variety shows didn't cover that cost and it never occurred to her to maybe raise ticket prices enough to allow for that needed expense. So she does what seems to her like the logical thing: She steals. Once a year, Zelda uses her stage magic to heist just enough cash to pay her supplier.

Eivol Eckdol runs the Gnome Bookstore in Gotham, but it's secretly a front for his real business of creating tricks for stage magicians. Since that's a perfectly legitimate real-world business, one wonders why he feels the need to keep it on the downlow but, hey, that's his choice. One also might feel as though he's gouging Zelda by overcharging her.

When we first see her, though, she's gathering her annual haul after apparently dynamiting her way into a bank vault. There's no alarm but a security guard shows up—an African-American, in fact, rare for this series outside of this episode. Zelda, wearing a gas mask, stands up when he tells her not to move and he immediately shoots her twice. Rather than fall down dead, she smacks him hard with her suitcase, presumably already counted out with an exact $100,000 in cash, and makes good her escape.

Was he a security guard or a police officer? His hat and the badge on his coat say "Police" but he's dressed more like a security guard. Either way, he was a bit trigger-happy and was presumably put on investigative leave afterwards.

Cut to Commissioner Gordon's office later that evening for a bit of exposition in which we learn of the annual pattern of these crimes. Gordon has his top men gathered—including another African-American actor. "Two years on this case," he chides, "And you men haven't turned up a single clue." Why they weren't expecting the robbery after the last two on the exact same date isn't addressed.

"This one is bigger than the lot of us," admits Chief O'Hara. "Commissioner, we need help." With that, they all turn toward the red "hot line" phone to Batman and Robin. Just in case it doesn't work, however, Gordon tells O'Hara to light up the Bat-Signal on the roof as well.

We're told—for no apparent reason—that the robbery took place at precisely 8:37pm. It must have taken some time to determine exactly how much money was taken so presumably it was at least pushing 11pm by the time the policemen were gathered at the office. Kind of late for Dick Grayson to be up on a school night and yet there he is, along with Bruce Wayne and ever-faithful butler Alfred (revived for television after having been killed off in the comics a couple years earlier) looking at stars and planets through a telescope. Dick's Aunt Harriet steps outside to promote the "delicious rib roast" she's cooked. Pretty late for a big meal like that, too. As she's looking around, though, enjoying the clear spring evening, she suddenly spots the Bat-Signal being flashed on the clouds...that aren't supposed to *be* there if it's a clear spring evening.

Quick thinking as always, Bruce suddenly "remembers" that he and Dick had tickets to a lecture on Latin American affairs and they race off, supposedly to try and catch part of it. By the time they were to get to town, it would likely be after midnight by that point! "Dick Grayson!" says the stunned Aunt Harriet, "Running out on a rib roast for a lecture in politics? Alfred, get ready to catch me. I think I'm going to faint!"

Meanwhile—as they say in comic books—Gordon is well aware of how late it's getting as he glances at his watch while sitting alone pressing the sole button on the glowing Batphone over and over. When Bruce finally *does* grab the beeping phone at stately Wayne

Manor, he says, "Sorry about the holdup, Commissioner. What's the problem?" Informed that a holdup *was* the problem, he doesn't wait for details.

For us the audience, we get to enjoy the awesomely cool Neal Hefti theme and all that great opening animation while we wait for them to arrive fully costumed in the Batcave and head out in the Batmobile via stock footage. Since this is a rare night trip, we even get to see the Batmobile's lights on.

The fact that it is a night trip also means that they couldn't use the stock footage of the Batmobile arriving at Police Headquarters with the same people walking down the steps episode after episode as the Caped Crusaders bound in. Instead, we get them going through the back parking lot of what gives the impression of a much smaller building and, even though they pass at least one empty parking spot as they drive up, our heroes just stop and get out, seemingly blocking a police car. In fact, two officers come out and open that car's door but never bother to ask Batman to move so they can get out!

Speaking of uncharacteristic behavior, with no leads whatsoever Batman and Robin decide that their next move is to *create* a lead. Gordon asks Robin how they were going to do that. "Don't worry!" replies the Boy Wonder, "Batman will figure it out!" Not sounding so sure, he then turns and asks, "Won't you, Batman?"

But the great detective, rather than detecting, plants a story in the early edition of the newspaper indicating that the robber got away with counterfeit money that was being stored at the bank to be destroyed. An aging newsboy (the great Frankie Darro, who was inside Robby the Robot in *Forbidden Planet!*) hawks the story the next morning right next to the gigantic poster of Zelda the Great. He even breaks the fourth wall at one point, addressing the camera. It wouldn't be the only time that happens in this episode.

Batman, being Batman, is able to determine that, as Robin put it, "the crook was a lady!"

"Hardly a lady, Robin, but female, yes," opines our hero.

At this point, Robin immediately suggests the Catwoman, a character who we wouldn't see on the air for several more episodes, but with whom the duo was obviously already familiar. Noting that she was "safely up the river," the Dark Knight presumes that they are instead, "facing some new super criminal, not in our crime file." The Commissioner later reacts to the news as if he's never heard of a woman criminal before. Not even Catwoman, Commish?

Finally, nearly halfway through the episode, we meet our orange-clad special guest villainess, arriving in a puff of orange smoke and Elton John shades in the back of Eckdol's bookstore, where he already has the money she had stolen. But he also has a copy of the morning paper with Batman's planted story.

The pair argues about the supposedly phony money and Eckdol plays on Zelda's neediness, enticing her by telling her about the sensational trap he had prepared for her that she now can't have because of this new turn of events. He reveals a cage constructed of "unbreakable jet-age plastic," and proceeds to shoot it multiple times with a semi-automatic weapon to prove his point.

The two of them go back and forth praising the doom trap, but Eckdol refuses to tell her the trick's secret until he gets his money. He does say that it involves Batman, whom he refers to as "the world's greatest escape artist," much to Zelda's jealous consternation.

We find out that the counterfeit money story wasn't the only story Batman planted. On the same page, there's an article about a rare emerald on display in Gotham. This doesn't go unnoticed by Eckdol, who tempts Zelda to steal it for his payment. The suspicious Zelda, though, worries that it "could be a typical Batman trap." So here we were thinking it was unusual for Batman to stoop to planting fake newspaper stories and yet Zelda seems familiar enough with his methods to refer to this as "typical."

She's right, of course. Batman and Robin are at the jewelry store delivering the fake emerald as the woman who owns the place swoons at the sight of the hunky hero. Misunderstanding completely and thinking she's put off by their costumes, Batman explains that, "This unique garb of ours is one of our weapons in crimefighting."

While the oblivious duo is setting things up, our orange villainess is watching it all with binoculars from across the street, even going so far as to comment directly to the viewer, "As I guessed, another Batman trap!" Knowing that the gem is now a setup, Zelda comes up with another way to get her money.

Batman, by the way, looks as if he could use a quick shave. Granted they've been on the go since this whole thing started. When do they sleep anyway? And how does Dick manage to stay in school, let alone find time for homework and studying? And where does Aunt Harriet think Dick is all the time?

Well, at this point, she apparently thought he was at a playground because she doesn't question for a second when a phone call from a "playground matron" informs her that he was hit with a batted ball and that a "special taxi" was coming to bring her to him.

In reality, Dick and Bruce—or at least their alter egos—are getting stiff and tired from hiding on a balcony at the jewelry store waiting for someone to steal the fake emerald. Finally, Zelda arrives, disguised in all black until she makes her play for the gem. Then she's her old, familiar, orange-clad self. Batman and Robin's stunt men leap down from the balcony and Zelda disappears! Batman, being Batman, immediately realizes that she "projected a false image with those tiny mirrors in her hat."

As they decide what to do next, the Commissioner reaches them via the Batmobile hotline to inform them that the criminal has kidnapped *Mrs. Harriet Cooper*—unbeknownst to him, Dick's Aunt Harriet!

As the episode ends, we see Zelda calmly knitting more of her trademark orange somethings as Aunt Harriet (or rather her stuntperson) is shown tied up in a straitjacket, walking on air, suspended above a vat of flaming oil, ready to be dropped without hesitation if Bruce Wayne doesn't pay $100,000 in exactly one hour!

She's still there, of course, when we return the next day—same bat time, same bat channel! But no sign of Bruce Wayne and time is ticking away. Robin is with the Chief and the Commissioner, waiting in frustration while Batman is supposedly out looking for Bruce. Nudge, nudge. Wink, wink. Why it's taking him so long I have no idea! Finally, twenty-five minutes into the hour, Bruce comes calmly striding into the office. Bruce is introduced to Chief O'Hara, which is interesting since they had already shared a scene in the earlier Joker episode! (In actuality, this gaffe was due to the fact that Zelda, actually the third episode shot, was pushed back to make room for what ABC, not yet aware of the phenomenon the series would be, felt were better episodes—the Joker and Mr. Freeze.)

Zelda has requested that contact be made via television so the Commissioner and Robin whisk Bruce down to the nearest station where a color Fox Western is interrupted to bring you a live black and white newsman before cutting away to the color Gordon. "Hello, criminals, wherever you are out there. Do you hear me criminals?" he asks. Zelda calls in and Robin tells her the truth about the supposed "counterfeit" money being real. She's excited by the news. Robin says, "Aw, come *on*, you crook! You can't be *all* bad! Let the poor lady go, huh?" And that's it. Zelda agrees to free Aunt Harriet, the Commissioner throws it back to the black and white anchor, who returns to the color Western movie, in progress.

We next see the blindfolded kidnap victim being dropped off back at Frankie Darro's downtown corner, right by Zelda's giant signage. Soon enough, she's back resting at Wayne Manor having been checked out by a doctor.

Bruce tells Alfred and the incredulous Robin that he has finally—almost halfway into the second part of the episode—deduced the identity of their opponent. Alfred, too, has come up with a clue as to where to find her: a book of matches advertising the Gnome Bookstore that had fallen out of Aunt Harriet's pocket. Since she doesn't smoke, and we know she had no idea where she was taken, it's obvious the matches were a plant. Still, our intrepid heroes head back to the Batmobile stock footage and leave the Batcave, only to end up in New York City's Times Square in 1962 based on the movies playing in the theaters they pass a couple of times in the background stock footage. Along the way, Batman finally informs Robin of the villain's identity.

Zelda and Eivol are happy with the $100,000 from the original bank robbery and she demands to know the secret of his doom trap...only to find out he doesn't have one. Instead, the goal all along has been to lure Batman into the trap and see how he—the world's greatest escape artist—gets out of it! Since Batman wouldn't be happy about their methods, Eckdol has also decided to make an extra $100,000 by selling the right to kill Batman to two mobsters. Hiding just outside the trap, once the Caped Crusader triumphantly survives it the two of them will shoot him before he even suspects they're there. The *fiends*!

Yeah, Zelda isn't thrilled with this turn of events, either. "Kidnapping! Murder! Where will it end? You know I abhor violence!" Still, she goes along, pointing out that having already deduced his plan, she had given the matches as a clue to lure Batman and Robin to the bookstore.

Eckdol takes control as the mob shooters (familiar character actors Victor French and William Phipps) arrive. He positions them inside two sarcophagi (found in all bookstores, naturally), each with machine gun slots. Batman and Robin finally arrive back in 1966 Gotham City and follow various clues to get to the doom trap, observed all the while by Eivol and Zelda from hiding. As the trap springs shut, Zelda bemoans, "It seems such a waste. They are such handsome creatures!"

Since Batman was expecting Zelda, he's probably surprised when Eivol's voice tells him about the trap they've wandered into. The Albanian brags that he's a genius and the Boy Wonder taunts back, "Yeah, that's what they *all* say!"

Trapped in the unbreakable plastic booth, with toxic gas coming from an electrified vent below, it looks like, as Robin says, "Curtains!" But Batman, being Batman, realizes that the gas must contain hydrogen and they use the metal from their belts to electrify it from the vent below and explode the chamber!

Eckdol is ecstatic and watches for the mobsters to kill the heroes only to have Zelda grab the mike and warn Batman and Robin, who duck, causing the crooks to shoot each other, making this one of only three episodes where anyone dies on the series.

In the end, Bruce Wayne visits Zelda in prison in her tight, slinky, striped prison outfit, complete with matching pillbox hat, and recommends special privileges for her since she saved Batman's life. He promises her when she gets out she can be "resident lady magician" at a children's hospital he owns. Zelda wiggles away after his visit, never to be seen again until she finally turns up in the comic books nearly fifty years down the line! Google it!

Steven Thompson aka Booksteve has written for Yoe Books, Bear Manor Media, Dark Horse, Fantagraphics, Twomorrows, and Time Capsule Productions, currently has 14 blogs, and is slowly working toward doing a regular podcast. His books include *The Best of Booksteve's Library* and (with actress Kathy Coleman), the award winning biography, *Run Holly Run!* Booksteve lives in Northern Kentucky with an understanding wife, a genius son, two cats that hate each other, a dog that minds her own business, and twenty-nine full bookcases.

ZOWIE!

Riddler's Return

"A Riddle a Day Keeps the Riddler Away/While the Rat's Away, the Mice Will Play"
By Chuck Dixon

There's a template to writing a successful Riddler story. This formula was worked out to perfection by the writers of the 1966 *Batman* series. They took the character's only two appearances in the comics (almost twenty years prior) and built upon that foundation to work out the *modus operandi* of Edward Nigma and set the course for other writers to follow to this day.

In the best Riddler tales, he confounds the Dynamic Duo by compulsively providing clues in the form of riddles or puzzles that both lead Batman and Robin to his latest caper and/or away from it depending on whether they provide the correct answers or not. I've often used *Die Hard with a Vengeance*, the Bruce Willis action movie, as the best example of a Riddler story that I know of. And, ironically, released the same summer as *Batman Forever*, a movie that actually featured the Riddler in a simply awful story that followed none of the indelible rules set down by Bill Finger in the comics as well as on the TV show.

The template's in place but the challenges are daunting. The riddles must both fit the crime as well as serving as red herrings. It can be a task and the reason why, while I love the Riddler as a character, I only featured him in a handful of stories during my eleven years writing Batman titles at DC Comics.

Here, in a pair of episodes that first aired in February of 1966, we have the first return of the Riddler to the small screen. This is his sophomore appearance after the unforgettable impression he created in the series' debut entries.

This time, the Prince of Puzzles seems more determined to lure our heroes into a deadly trap than to simply lead them on a wild goose chase. He figures, with the pesky pair dead, he'll have free reign to create mayhem in Gotham with a scheme to extort one million dollars from the city's coffers.

The first episode of our story begins with the arrival of King Boris in Gotham. He's a splendidly gracious ruler from an unnamed country enjoying a friendly relationship with the USA. He's in town to present a gem studded replica of the Queen of Liberty statue that sits in Gotham Harbor, though we never actually see the original, multi-story, statue *in situ* in the episode. An ambitious effects shot out of reach of the show's budget, probably. He's met at the airport by dignitaries, the press and a precocious young thing dressed as a schoolgirl who presents Boris with a bouquet of flowers. The flowers explode in sparks and smoke and launch a projectile from which a parachute drops with a banner suspended below it with the riddle in gold lettering on an, appropriately, purple cloth.

"When is a person like a piece of wood?"

This simple quiz, that probably had 90% of the kids watching shouting out the answer, has Commissioner Gordon and Chief O'Hara total flummoxed. They turn, of course to the Batphone.

But, with his hand on the phone, Gordon has a mini-soliloquy in which he wonders about Batman's true identity and confesses that he resists thinking more about the Dark Knight's alter ego because "we owe him that much." The show's producers and writers, once again, neatly work out one of the imponderables of Batman. If Gordon's such a great cop then why can't he figure out who Batman and Robin are? In this iteration, it is a willing blindspot Gordon has created. This reveal will play a part later in our story and is probably why this little bit of exposition occurs early on.

Bruce Wayne interrupts a chess game with his young ward to respond to the urgent call and, after a brief encounter with Aunt Harriett, he and Dick rush to the Batpoles. It's off to Gotham with a roar of the Batmobile's rocket engine!

Down in the bowels of the sewers, the Riddler schemes and preens before his newly recruited gang, the River Rats. His cunning initial plan is to have the Caped Crusader run himself ragged all over town chasing after the clues found in the riddles.

At police HQ, Batman and Robin do some Olympian logic-leaping. Surely the answer to the first riddle is "When he's a ruler." A reference to King Boris, no doubt? Perhaps the Riddler means to steal the golden replica of the Queen of Liberty.

Being a fair-minded gentleman, Batman points out that the clue might just as well refer to a woman. He also uses his past experience with Nigma to surmise that the crook wouldn't waste his efforts on a statue worth only tens of thousands. A greater prize would be the diamond-encrusted tiara to be awarded at the Queen of Beauty pageant that very night!

The Dynamic Duo is in attendance at the contest that evening and watch as the Riddler brazenly plucks the glittering crown right from the teased hair of the winning lovely. The giggling felon escapes into the sewers but not before leaving behind a fresh puzzler.

"What room can no man enter?"

Again, imagine thousands of little wiseasses all over the USA calling out the answer in their living rooms.

Batman has a nice bit of dialogue here where he explains to Robin that, so long as the riddles keep coming, the Riddler's plan is still in motion. When the riddles stop, that means Nigma's crime is about to go down. The nature of this bit of schooling is written in a way that intimates that Batman had an encounter or two with the Riddler in his pre-Robin days. Man, I love finding stuff like that in these episodes.

As any snotnose ten-year old in 1966 could tell you, a mushroom is a room no man can enter. That makes it patently obvious that the target is King Boris after all as the unsuspecting suzerain is attending dinner at Gotham's Royal Mushroom Club! The Duo catches up with Boris in the club's wine cellar where they draw him aside to warn him of the terrible danger he's in. The spot they choose for their *tete-a-tete* leaves Boris standing on a trap door that even the club's oldest members have never seen before.

Down the trap the king goes along with his closely guarded replica of the Queen of Liberty.

But, as we learn, Batman has placed a tracking device in the purloined tiara. He and Robin will track follow his electronic signal; right into the Riddler's hidey hole and nab the mincing miscreant and free King Boris.

The Riddler quickly discovers that the priceless trinket he stole from the hottie's blonde tresses is just a worthless replica made of paste. He broods a bit for the cheap seats as, in a shot that was pretty complex for the small screen in that day, Batman and Robin slip in through a hatchway in the background.

Of course, as we are drawing toward the twenty-five minute mark of this episode, it all turns out to be an elaborate trap. Batman and Robin are felled by a weighted net that drops them to the floor. In a further humiliation, Riddler's gangs sprays them with slippery, sticky gunk that makes it impossible for them stand up or get a grip on anything.

Riddler takes some time to gloat and actually references the Joker, Mister Freeze, and the Penguin. He graciously acknowledges that they have "skills" but now he's proven that Edward Nigma is the true king of crime.

For the cliffhanger, the Dynamic Duo find themselves tied spread-eagle over the mouths of massive industrial air vents. When the vents go on, our heroes will spin with the fan blades. The Riddler makes the gruesome promise that the centrifugal force created will strip their flesh from their bones. That's a bit much. Brain hemorrhages would be more likely. And so, they are left to spin to their graves as the Riddler and his River Rats make their exit. And we are urged to return the following night.

The next episode begins with Batman and Robin spinning like airplane props until a junction box behind Batman explodes in sparks and his fan slows to a stop, as does Robin's. He frees himself so easily it made me wonder why he hadn't previously. Batman then frees the unconscious Boy Wonder and, after bringing him around with a few stern words of encouragement, explains how he escaped the trap in a way that bears no relationship to what actually happened.

I had to wind back to see if what Batman was saying made any sense at all. It didn't. I never saw him free a hand and pull an acetylene torch from his utility belt. And the fuse box in question was behind him and far out of reach. Was his escape pure dumb luck and he told Robin this whopper to add to his crimefighting cred?

More likely, they simply couldn't film the sequence as written but went on with the existing dialogue anyway. Hell, it's not like anyone could do an instant replay, right? And by the time it was re-run that summer, who'd remember to look out for it?

Traps are a bitch to write, trust me. And this poor crew formatted a series with a new trap every week for three seasons! I give them fourteen miles of slack.

So, the Dynamic Duo is back on the case. But the world at large believes they're dead. The Riddler thinks he's living in a Batman-free world now and it's clear sailing to his masterpiece caper.

Only the abduction of King Boris turns out to be a ruse as the king is eventually released to the safekeeping of Gotham PD. Even the replica statuette of the Queen of Liberty is returned and finds its place in the museum located at the very top of the full-sized Queen of Liberty statue.

The surprises mount higher as the Riddler has, unsuspected by all, placed a bomb inside the statuette and threatens to blow up this proud symbol of democracy unless he receives a million dollars in cold cash. The city can't raise that kind of bread and so turns to Gordon's "good friend" millionaire socialite Bruce Wayne.

Bruce delivers the ransom himself and is happy to do so even as Gordon assures him it's "only a loan." And who should arrive to pick up the satchel of loot but Batman! What the hell? Bruce Wayne and Batman in the same room?

It quickly becomes apparent that this "Batman" is none other than Whitey of the River Rat Gang. His attempts to mimic Batman's manner of speaking and body language wouldn't fool even Chief O'Hara. Bruce takes it all in his usual unflappable way and never lets on, except for a few wry replies upon meeting this fraud. Bruce remarks that he's always wanted to meet Batman. Whitey assures him that the feeling is mutual. There's a crunch sound effect as they shake hands and we see Whitey wincing and trying to cover up the pain of Bruce's vise-like grip. Before departing out a convenient window, the ersatz Dark Knight assures one and all that he and Robin will be at the exchange and "jump into action" once the bomb has been deactivated. Bruce adds his two cents "as a layman" to advise Gordon that this sounds like a solid plan.

The cops deliver the goods to Riddler who has, inexplicably, decided that the museum at the Queen of Liberty would be good place for the exchange. The punchline becomes an *ouch*line when the bag of cash explodes in confetti and Batman and Robin arrive very much alive to the Riddler's chagrin. Their entrance is a clever one as they leap through a life-size poster of themselves on permanent display in the museum. Batman informs the gang, and the viewers, that he saw through the Riddler's chicanery and has already defused the bomb.

A punch-up ensues and soon all the hoods are kicked, knocked and bludgeoned into submission just as the Gotham cops roll in to slap on the cuffs.

The episode ends with Aunt Harriett announcing that she's off with some out-of-town friends to tour the new exhibit at the Queen of Liberty. She invites the boys to come along but Bruce begs off with something about work he has to do with the Wayne Foundation and Dick says he has to study for an algebra test.

Well, Bruce may have told a little white lie but he insists that Dick hit the math book and the story closes.

Frank Gorshin returns as the Riddler after his brash, lunatic and daring portrayal in the premiere outings. Maybe he rethought things by the time it came to be in these episodes. The show had not aired yet so there was no kind of public reaction to his first appearance. It looks here like he decided to dial it back a bit. There's not so much of a mad capering and grand gesturing this time. He's still way over the top but slightly more subdued here. He looks to be going for a more noirish performance filled with menace. This lends itself to the most often used sets in these episodes which are in claustrophobia-inducing sewers and tunnels. Lots of deep shadows and confined spaces. Gorshin draws us in rather than reaching out for us. He uses his Rod Steiger over-enunciation more here than his Tommy Udo giggle. He has a very effective super close-up which he ends by breaking the fourth wall to stare into the eyes of the audience. In other words, still stealing every scene but in a different way.

Another reason he might have turned down the volume is the very silly nature of his henchmen in this story. This time out he has adopted the River Rat Gang, Whiskers, Whitey and Fang. Three strange characters who wear hoodies in different primary colors and spend their days munching cheese and taking on the body language of rodents. Along with them is Mousey, a squeaky-voiced moll who alternately dresses in a private school uniform or in a kind of preppy go-go chic. Whitey is played by Roy Jensen who specialized in playing thugs and was often shot, beaten or otherwise abused by Clint Eastwood in many films. Jensen is all-in for the silliness and appears to be having a great time in his scenes as the faux-Batman; even correcting himself when he refers to the Gotham PD as "cops."

The selection of the River Rats here may directly have inspired and informed my own portrayals of the Riddler in comic scripts I've written. The Joker and the Penguin are a dangerous psychotic and a forceful personality, respectively. One can see how these two might hold a gang together through fear and intimidation. And the allure of being one of Catwoman's henchmen is obvious.

But the Riddler comes off as an unhinged loser for the most part. I always imagined that he'd need to scrape the bottom of Gotham's criminal barrel for recruits. Who better than a gang who live in a drain pipe and whose biggest heist would be from the dairy department at the Gotham Supermart? These are the kind of shiftless nitwits even Eddie Nigma could push around.

Reginald Denny is on hand as King Boris. A former matinee idol of the 1930s, Denny was a mainstay on radio and television through the 50s and 60s. He had a recurring role as Reggie the Butler on the *Red Skeleton Show*. He would also return as Commodore Schmidlapp for the Batman feature film. For all you real trivia nuts, Denny was also an avid aviation nut and former RAF fighter pilot in the Great War as well as an inventor. He helped create a radio-controlled drone used to train anti-aircraft crews in WWII. Holy Cutting Edge! And, of course, in these episodes he gives King Boris just the right touch of pomp and bluster.

It's still early in the series and, while the played-straight, satiric tone is already well in place, everyone in the main cast is still working out the nuances of their performances. Burt Ward approaches his role with almost the same gusto here as he will for the rest of the run.

But Adam West is still finding his way a bit. His performance is spot-on here but lacks some of the indefatigable authority he would develop over time. In these episodes, he's given little opportunity for arch one-liners played with the fine line between ham-acting and parody that he will eventually absolutely master. There is simply not another actor in the world who could be so grave and so silly simultaneously. Was he aware that this would play to two separate audiences who would appreciate it on two entirely different levels? He had to, right? You don't walk into a role like this without a whole lot of thought. Even so, the guy was fearless in his commitment.

And I imagine that, once they saw what West was capable of, the writers wrote to his strengths. What a great talent to write lines for. In these episodes there's a lost opportunity when the apparently jailbait-aged Mousey shows an undue level of attraction to Batman. West plays it oblivious at first and then is a bit flustered as he feels the heat off her. It's well played but not as much is made of the scene as it would be in similar encounters with femme fatales later on. Catwoman would be along four episodes later and the writers have a field day there with West showing off the befuddled beau routine in all its red-faced glory.

Also, a sure sign that we're in early days, there's a Batman and Robin wall climb that features no celebrity cameo. There's also only one Zap! Pow! Whammo! fist fight as the Duo and the River Rats only come face to face on a level playing field one time in the story. And the fight ends with some colorful animated action and pain marks coming from Whitey's head as he sinks into unconsciousness. I may stand corrected, but I don't recall that happening in a lot of later episodes.

Another interesting feature is the extensive use of the Bat-computer as Batman and Robin do a search for the likely location for the Riddler's hideout as provided by one of his riddles. They use a primitive version of Google Maps which is pretty much nothing more than a slide show. But still advanced thinking for 1966 and years away from the first computer monitors let alone image storage. This was still the punch card age, after all.

These episodes were written by Fred De Gorter who would script two other episodes. Not terribly prolific, he wrote a couple of forgettable B films, an episode of *Daniel Boone* and a Mr. Magoo cartoon.

Director Tom Gries, however, would go on to create the WWII action series *The Rat Patrol* and later direct numerous TV episodes and features including the classic western film *Will Penny* as well as the TV movie of *Helter Skelter*, about the real-life Manson Family murders.

All in all, a worthy outing for the Prince of Puzzlers and another fun, fast paced adventure for Gotham's favorite sons.

Born and raised in Philadelphia, **Chuck Dixon** worked a variety of jobs from driving an ice cream truck to working graveyard at a 7-11 before trying his hand as a writer. After a brief sojourn in children's books he turned to his childhood love of comic books. In his thirty years as a writer for Marvel, DC Comics and other publishers, Chuck built a reputation as a prolific and versatile freelancer working on a wide variety titles and genres from Conan the Barbarian to SpongeBob. His graphic novel adaptation of J.R.R. Tolkien's *The Hobbit* continues to be an international bestseller translated into fifty languages. He is the co-creator (with Graham Nolan) of the Batman villain Bane, the first enduring member added to the Dark Knight's rogues gallery in forty years. He was also one of the seminal writers responsible for the continuing popularity of Marvel Comics' The Punisher.

After making his name in comics, Chuck moved to prose in 2011 and has since written over twenty novels, mostly in the action-thriller genre with a few side-trips to horror, hardboiled noir and western. The transition from the comics form to prose has been a life-altering event for him. As Chuck says, "writing a comic is like getting on a roller coaster while writing a novel is more like a long car trip with a bunch of people you'll learn to hate." His Levon Cade novels are currently in production as a television series from Sylvester Stallone's Balboa Productions. He currently lives in central Florida and, no, he does not miss the snow.

ZOK!

13 Thoughts on 13 Hats

"The Thirteenth Hat/Batman Stands Pat"
By Dan Greenfield

There's this thing we do at the website 13th Dimension: We count in increments of thirteen. Why have a Top Ten list when we can have a Top Thirteen? Why show off ten favorite comic-book covers when we can show you thirteen? And why, when ruminating on a particular subject, should we share TEN QUICK THOUGHTS when thirteen is even better? (Though I admit I sometimes wish we were, say, 8th Dimension.)

Now, the editor of this fine publication had the presence of mind to assign me "The Thirteenth Hat" (and its concluding segment "Batman Stands Pat") for my contribution to the book. So, I just figured I'd do him one better by cribbing the THIRTEEN QUICK THOUGHTS format—though these thoughts aren't exactly "quick"—as opposed to crafting a more linear episode-guide entry. The way I figure it, if you're reading this book, chances are very high that you already know how this episode goes. Rather, it's all about the details.

So, here goes:

1. Thirteens All Around. "The Thirteenth Hat" is, coincidentally or not, the thirteenth episode of the series and, with its flip side "Batman Stands Pat," the seventh story of the season. The two parts aired Feb. 23 and 24, 1966, and introduced another comics villain to the show's audience: Jervis Tetch, the Mad Hatter.

The plot is simultaneously simple and—central to the show's campy conceit—needlessly complex: The Hatter plans to steal the hats of the twelve jurors who sent him to prison—and the jurors themselves. His aim? To ransom them off for a collection of presidential hats worth—as Tetch crows a la Dr. Evil—"millions."

But the capper of the plot is the Hatter's scheme to purloin Batman's cowl—the titular "Thirteenth Hat"—as revenge for the Caped Crusader's damning trial testimony. Without his cowl, Tetch reasons, Batman's identity will be exposed and he'll be ruined as an ace crimefighter.

2. Comics Roots. The episode bears the hallmarks of a Season One installment: It's colorful without being garish and campy without being too broad. That said, it's not quite as entertaining as the better-known Season Two follow-up "The Contaminated Cowl" and its wonderfully wacky pink Batman mask.

But like many of Season One's early eps, the two-parter is bolstered by being a straight adaptation of the source material: Writer Charles Hoffman and director Norman Foster took their cues from at least two comics—primarily *Batman* #161's "The New Crimes of the Mad Hatter," by writer Dave Wood, penciller Sheldon Moldoff and inker Charles Paris (cover-dated February 1964) and, secondarily, *Detective Comics* #230's "The Mad Hatter of Gotham City," by Batman co-creator Bill Finger, Moldoff and Paris (cover-dated April 1956).

It makes sense: *Batman* #161 came out not long before the show went into production and the story from *Detective* #230 was reprinted in *Batman Annual* #3, cover-dated Summer 1962. So, it wasn't like the producers had to look far for inspiration.

Of the two issues, the overall plot of "The Thirteenth Hat" strongly mirrors "The New Crimes of the Mad Hatter," with its juror/hat-kidnapping scheme. The ep's sculptor subplot, however, is lifted from "The Mad Hatter of Gotham City." (That story actually provided the framework for the aforementioned "The Contaminated Cowl"—also written by Hoffman.)

3. A Great Villain Who Could Have Been Bigger. Fewer villains on the series were cast better than the Mad Hatter. David Wayne is a dead ringer for Jervis Tetch as he appeared on the page—with his bright red wig and mustache and bushy, black eyebrows.

Nattily attired in his light gray top hat and tails, Wayne minces about, over-enunciating "Byatman" as he chews the scenery with malefic intent. (Leaving no cliché unturned, he even mimes twirling his mustache at one point.)

And it's the outlandish power of Wayne's performance that makes the Mad Hatter so memorable: The villain only showed up twice across the series, but his appearances stand out—and fans were justifiably pleased when the actor's likeness was included in the Batman Classic TV Series merchandise deal struck in 2012. You can now get David Wayne Mad Hatter action figures, sculptures and other ephemera.

Yet Wayne himself disliked the role, according to Joel Eisner's *The Official Batman Batbook*. By the time *Batman* premiered in 1966, Wayne had been a respected actor for nearly thirty years and his career would stretch forward for decades more. (He won the first-ever Tony for Best Actor in a Featured Role/Musical in 1947 for *Finian's Rainbow* and won a second Tony in 1954 for Best Actor/Play in *The Teahouse of the August Moon.*)

But the show's popularity—and its endurance in syndication—meant that a lot of fans knew him best for his over-the-top performance on *Batman*, even if he had no desire to repeat his Season One appearance.

"It was too tough to get me to do a second one," Wayne once said, according to the *Batbook*. "They held a gun to my head to do it. They had already written a script for the Mad Hatter, and I said I wouldn't do it. So, they used all the strength of the studio in order to force me to do it. Finally, I just gave in. I just thought it was cheap and, beneath me, really, as a performer. But strangely enough, most of the fan mail I get is from people who knew and loved *Batman* and new kids who still see it."

4. Lisa, that Classy Dame. The villains' molls throughout the series are kind of a mixed bag, some more standout than others, owing not just to a particular actress' skill but how much they're given to do. Most, it's pretty clear, were cast for their sex appeal, as opposed to their acting chops.

Diane McBain's Lisa ranks among the better ones: The actress brings a refined air to the proceedings, looking like she arrived on set directly from the local country club, with her tasteful pearls and skirt ensemble. She also has a central role in the Hatter's scheme—as the inside woman at Madame Magda's hat shop and as an operative charged with getting Turkey Bullwinkle to give up the location of his bowler hat, which Tetch needs to complete his collection.

Like most of the molls and their villainous leaders, her relationship with the Mad Hatter is strictly asexual—she and Tetch have strong chemistry, but you never for a second think of them as a couple. (Come to think of it, only Frank Gorshin's Riddler gave off the vibe that he was sleeping with the women in his various gangs.)

Rather, the two come off as friends and colleagues. If I were to invent a back story for her, I'd say she's a bored socialite who got wrapped up with the Hatter because it seemed like a fun thing to do—and because she's morally bankrupt. In essence, she's a smarter version of Season Two's Baby Jane Towser.

McBain's aristocratic bearing served her well with *Batman*'s producers, too. She was brought back in the second season to play the more flamboyant Pinky Pinkston in the famed Green Hornet two-parter.

5. That's a Lot of Exclamation Points!!! The episode gives us two Batfights: the first at sculptor Octave Marbot's studio at the end of Part One, and the second at the hat factory toward the finish of Part Two.

The sound effects? Well, the first one gave us ZAP! BOFF!, ZLOTT!, CRASH! and ZLOPP!

And the second featured BAM!, ZOK!!, POW!, KAPOW!, BIFF! the oddly inscrutable PAM!, THUNK! and WHAMM!!

Oh, and ZZZZZWAP! — with five Zs!

6. Alfred Joins In. It was a kick whenever Alfred (Alan Napier) got involved directly with whatever case Batman was working on, whether it meant dressing up as the Caped Crusader or hopping on his own Alfcycle.

In Part Two of this episode, Batman tasks Alfred with getting Turkey Bullwinkle's hat and placing inside it a tracking device so the Dynamic Duo can follow the Mad Hatter back to his hideaway.

Alfred proudly agrees with a resolute, "If I may be allowed, sir: Roger!"

And off he goes to Bullwinkle's Bowladrome, where he poses as a genealogist, of all things, to convince Turkey (George Conrad) to tell him where his hat is—so that Alfred can inspect it for clues to his lineage.

It's a preposterous ruse the show plays straight—which was one of the series' greatest strengths in the first season. The whole thing is inherently absurd, but you buy it because everyone on screen does—even Turkey, as perplexed as he is. (By the way, Conrad reminds me of a befuddled Arthur Fonzarelli for some reason.)

7. Utter Nonsense. There's a term that's thrown around a lot on John S. Drew's essential *Batcave Podcast*: Gotham City Logic. It's the idea that *Batman* episodes have a relentless tendency to ignore gigantic plot holes by, well, ignoring them. Or have Batman and Robin draw important conclusions without any real or plausible—and often contradictory—information.

It's all because *Batman* is what it is: An entertaining parody that challenges you to make sense of nonsense because it has no desire to make sense of it itself. A major underpinning of the show is that rational plot structure often has to be sacrificed in the name of absurdism. Otherwise, where's the joke?

So, I'm often amused when I see people get annoyed that something in a *Batman* episode doesn't make sense. That's because it's not supposed to: There's gold in them thar camp mines.

In "The Thirteenth Hat," there are three especially notable examples. At the risk of over-explaining the joke:

* The Mad Hatter wants revenge on the twelve jurors who convicted him. So how come none—save Turkey Bullwinkle in Part Two— recognize Tetch when he approaches them to steal their hats?

It's because it's a lot more amusing to have the Hatter go after them with his "super instant mesmerizer" without having them scream in horror and try to make a break for it. Besides, we have to see the villain at work before we're allowed to understand his evil scheme. Having everyone recognize him would throw that into disarray.

* Then there's the scene at Madame Magda's after the shop owner is taken by Tetch. Lisa hands Batman and Robin a card that was supposedly left behind, with Octave Marbot's name on it. But instead of going straight to the studio, our two heroes hightail it all the way back to the Batcave, where they figure out that Marbot is next on the Hatter's list.

Without the Batcave scene, however, we'd get no visit to the ever-popular Giant Lighted Lucite Map of Gotham City—and the episode would be poorer for it: Sure they could have gone directly to Marbot's, but where's the fun in that?

* Then there's the scene in the second part (again in the Batcave) where Batman finally figures out Tetch's scheme, even though he should have had it nailed down within ten minutes of his first call from Commissioner Gordon. (That all the victims were jurors in a case he was directly involved in would not have escaped Batman's notice for that long.)

Still, without Batman's circuitous investigation, you wouldn't have gotten this hilarious deadpan exchange, when the solution finally comes to the Caped Crusader:

Batman: "How could I have been so stupid?"
Robin: "All in all, Batman, you've been pretty busy."

Yeah, pretty busy chasing his own tail, thanks to the production team. Yet that's Gotham City Logic, folks: Logic need not apply.

8. Bursting at the Bat-Seams. Adam West generally played Batman as cool and straight. Excitable declarations were generally left to Burt Ward and Robin.

But once the Caped Crusader figures out the Mad Hatter's plot, he's so whipped up, he cries out loudly that he's found, "the key that will hoist our opponent on his own petard!"

West delivers the line with such gusto that you can't help burst out laughing at Batman's uncommonly forceful bravado.

9. Batman, the Closet Fascist. It's worth noting, by the way, that a more typical Batman pronouncement comes early in Part One, as the heroes are gathered in Gordon's office.

Now, the Caped Crusader was generally portrayed as so straight that you take his viewpoint as a road map to proper living. Except sometimes you have to read between the lines.

As the Dynamic Duo prepares to pursue the Mad Hatter, Gordon—in his customarily obsequious way—expresses gratitude that Batman's on the job.

"Fighting crime deserves no gratitude," Batman humbly replies. "It's my fervent hope that warped minds such as his can be rehabilitated once and for all."

I wonder if Batman ever read *A Clockwork Orange*.

(Speaking of, Gordon himself laments earlier in the episode, "It was a sad day indeed when the word 'parole' was coined.")

10. Conspiracy Theories and Libidinous Ladies. The *Batman* writers often made sly political references and this episode is no exception.

When Batman and Robin arrive at Madame Magda's hat shop after the proprietor was kidnapped, they question one of the customers, Hermione Monteagle (Norma Varden), who, thanks to prevalent Cold War hysteria, believes that an international conspiracy is at play:

"You know, I'm sure the communists had something to do with this," she tells the Caped Crusaders.

"I suspect the culprit can be found closer to home, Mrs. Monteagle," Batman gently corrects her.

"Hermione," she breathlessly replies.

Mrs. Monteagle isn't the only one clearly smitten with Batman, by the way. There's also Babette, the hat-check girl at the firemen's convention, where another hatnapping's taken place.

Played by Sandra Wells (who sounds like she was fighting off a head cold), Babette practically throws herself at the Masked Manhunter, though he, as usual, only has eyes for Lady Justice.

Meanwhile, the producers really pushed the envelope with the double-entendres.

As William Dozier narrates the opening to "Batman Stands Pat," he refers to Lisa as "a dish." Then, a moment or two later, Babette pops up on screen, followed by Madame Magda's kidnapping:

"Another dish," Dozier says excitedly. "And another snatch!"

11. Holy Gadgets! What is Batman without his gadgets, I ask you. And what is *Batman* without them, as well?

A lot less colorful, that's for sure.

"The Thirteenth Hat" doesn't get too crazy with Batman's array of crimefighting tools—the Mad Hatter's hat tops them all in this one—but there are a number of groovy selections.

Among the better ones are the aforementioned Giant Lighted Lucite Map of Gotham City, which is always a welcome sight. There's also the Batmobile's Anti-Theft Activator and the classic Detect-a-Scope.

But perhaps the best—i.e., silliest—is the one that fails when Batman needs it most: The Anti-Mesmerizing Bat-Reflector—which is just a mirror shaped like a bat that the Caped Crusader tries to use to deflect the beams from Tetch's top hat while they face off against each other at Marbot's studio.

Batman catches the beam and the mirror returns fire—right into Robin's eyes.

"Holy ricochet!" The Boy Wonder yelps, keeling over.

"Robin! Old chum!" Batman calls out—allowing the Mad Hatter to get the jump on our hero and push him under a pipe of "super-fast hardening plaster."

Deathtrap!

12. Murder by Death. The episode actually gives us two legit deathtraps: the one at the studio and the one at Hatter's warehouse.

The one at the studio is visually appealing—the gigantic plaster Bat-lump looks cool—but it's pretty low-fi and relatively uninspired, as those early in Season One often were.

Even worse is Batman's explanation how he survived suffocation before breaking out of the plaster: He just held his breath. You could argue that such simplicity is the point of the gag, but it feels like a missed opportunity. (Robin, on the other hand, is impressed: "Holy frogman!" he exclaims.)

The Hatter's hat-factory machinery, on the other hand, is certainly among the nastier ideas the show's producers came up with. Its collection of "flailing knives" (helpfully identified by a sign on the machine) and other blades is actually intimidating. But the construction of the machine prop is so shoddy—the show's set builders get rare marks off—that it never really lives up to its promise.

And the Hatter's hideout itself is cramped and rather lifeless and dismal.

All in all, both the deathtraps and the lair come up short.

13. Seeing the Future. David Wayne was given a ton of room to do his thing—and one of his best bits is the scene at Marbot's studio where the Mad Hatter disguises himself as the artist, complete with beret and faux Van Dyke.

What sells it though, is Wayne's absurdly thick French accent: "I don't know ze Mad Hatter. I am Octave Marbot, a simple sculptor," he claims to a skeptical Batman.

But no scene better encapsulates the Hatter's madness—and Wayne's commitment to the gag, his distaste notwithstanding—than his brief soliloquy toward the end of "Batman Stands Pat," where he stands near his hat-factory machinery and fantasizes about what he wants to do to the Caped Crusader.

"Why, I'll make him into a sun bonnet! Or a ten-gallon hat!" he calls out. "Or a fez! A fez! Yes, a fez!

"I'll dye him red. I'll buy myself a camel and go riding off into the desert, wearing a tribal chieftain's flowing robes—and Batman on my head."

"He's flipped his lid," Cappy the henchman (Roland La Starza) rightfully mutters to his partner Dicer (Gil Perkins).

Of course, the Hatter would indeed don a red fez in Hoffman's second season "The Contaminated Cowl"—so there's a little Bat-foreshadowing for you.

"The Thirteenth Hat," is a solid, if unspectacular, addition to the series. It even gets its own little milestone: For the first time at the cliffhanger—as pointed out at Tor.com by writer Keith R.A. DeCandido—both Dozier's voiceover and the screen text say "Same Bat-time!! Same Bat-Channel!!" It's a small thing, but notable nonetheless.

In any event, they say a hero is only as good as his villain. In this case, I'd extend that to an entire episode: "The Thirteenth Hat" isn't a Top Thirteen episode—it didn't make 13th Dimension's count-down—but, without a doubt, David Wayne's Mad Hatter was a top-flight bad guy.

Dan Greenfield is the editor and publisher of 13th Dimension, a website that celebrates comics yesterday and today. He first watched *Batman* when it was in syndication in the early '70s on New York's Channel 11, and over the years he's chronicled the history and legacy of the show, including interviews with Adam West, Burt Ward and Julie Newmar. He counts his flights on Eugene Nock's original 1966 Batcopter among the highlights of his charmed Bat-life, as his wife, Wendy, calls it. Dan and Wendy have a grown son, Sam, and they live with their cats Lex and Zod. Maybe next time, they'll name their pets Joker and Penguin.

ZLONK!

Wealth, Wayward Teens, and Wards

"The Joker Goes to School/He Meets His Match, the Grisly Ghoul"
By Kevin Dilmore & Dayton Ward

Riddle us this: Why is the United States in the 1960s like Bruce Wayne? Its veneer of civility, stability and upstanding citizenry roiled internally and continually against itself. From within, cries for freedom and justice pushed back against established social practices. Evolving moral codes resulted in weighing, disregarding, and often breaking rules in favor of what was perceived to be truly just, right, and fair.

Sound like someone we know?

Our mental pictures of this storied decade of American history can be as radically different as a playboy philanthropist is from a caped crusader. Seeing flashbacks to youth-driven oppositional movements, counterculture lifestyles, and clashes with law enforcement? We may want that to define "The Sixties," but that's more indicative of the latter years of the decade—and equally applicable to much of the first half of the 1970s. Throwing a dart at visions of the 1960s, particularly those provided by network television at the time, is more likely to hit a tie-sporting, white-collar white guy with an upwardly mobile gig; the sort of man who comes from a hard day at the office to a well-kept home in the suburbs, a loving family, and a cool, sporty ride.

You know ... like Bruce Wayne.

For many of these good-guy protagonists (think of them as more "Mad Men" than Mod Men), life was good. When existential threats presented themselves, they oftentimes did so in the unpredictable form of youth: boys and girls who, representing change from the status quo, threatened unruly and chaotic behavior, spat contempt for adults, and showed disdain for everything grown-ups had worked—*worked!*—to achieve.

So it went in Gotham City circa 1966, when the Clown Prince of Crime himself, the Joker, enlisted a group of high-school dropouts and a greed-driven cheerleader in a scheme to win a million-dollar wager. It's all chronicled in the *Batman* first-season two-parter, "The Joker Goes to School" and "He Meets His Match, the Grisly Ghoul," that aired March 2-3, 1966. Featuring the second series appearance by Batman's arch enemy and written by Lorenzo Semple, Jr., *Batman* series co-developer and executive story and script consultant, the relatively straightforward and nearly fight-free story—the only slugfest occurs in the final minutes—exists on the cusp of a shift in direction for television's depiction of teen antagonists. The two-bit, shiftless thugs depicted in this slice of *Batman* would in series and seasons to come give way to more dire and arguably more credible threats to society.

"The Joker Goes to School" opens at Gotham City's Woodrow Roosevelt High School, and we the audience are introduced to students in the gymnasium who are participating in basketball or cheerleading practice and—in the case of young Dick Grayson—weight training. Wrapping up their practice, three of the cheerleaders opt to take a break by grabbing some milk from the nearby vending machine. When Susie, the head cheerleader, deposits a dime for her selection, the machine instead provides five silver dollars. Holy return on investment!

After other students receive the same payout, school administrators do what you would normally do in this situation: call Gotham City Police Headquarters! There, Commissioner Gordon quickly deduces the students are victims of a bizarre joke, which can only mean the Joker! Certain they've only seen the Clown Prince of Crime's opening move in a much larger scheme, Gordon reaches out to Batman. Even before the world's greatest detective can begin his investigation, another school vending machine has acted up. This time it's a candy machine, dispensing negotiable stocks and bonds.

Meanwhile, in a swanky little bar across town, a jukebox offers up the Joker's sinister laugh along with a double-barrel shotgun instead of records, holding the patrons at bay so a pair of the Joker's masked henchmen can clean out the cash register.

Rushing to the school, Batman meets with members of the student council, including head cheerleader Susie and council president Dick Grayson. He warns the students the Joker may be attempting to lure them into a self-destructive pattern of "easy living," during which they'll give up on their studies and drop out of school. This would make them prime candidates for recruitment by criminals such as the Joker.

The students initially balk at this idea, unwilling to see anything sinister in what is surely a simple bit of good fortune thrown their way. Even before Batman arrives on the scene, Dick has tried to alert his friends of the possible danger, but they discount his concerns because what does he know? He's the ward of a famous millionaire and already enjoying the easy life, so how can he possibly understand their struggles? One might argue Susie and the others have a point. Come to think of it, why is Dick Grayson even attending a public school in the first place? Is this a deliberate aspect of his upbringing Bruce Wayne opted to follow, thereby making sure his young ward doesn't grow up within the same bubble of privilege he did? It's an interesting notion, but of course this is one of those little details the series never really finds time to address.

No sooner does Batman invoke the Joker's name and shows the students his mug shots than he appears as if from thin air itself! Though the Joker denies any wrongdoing, Batman still attempts to arrest him for loitering on school property. Unfortunately, the Joker seems to know the law better than Batman, in that one can only be deemed a loiterer if they remain in the same place for more than two minutes. Curses! Batman is foiled!

Later, we learn the Joker has established his new hideout in an abandoned garage behind the "Easy Living Candy Store," which he's filled with assets from the One-Armed Bandit Novelty Company he recently purchased. There, he meets with high-school dropouts Nick and Two-Bits, the henchmen of his new "Bad Pennies" gang, as they plan the next steps of his caper. Joining them is Susie, who's also a member of the gang. Holy turncoat! Susie's managed to get her hands on the answers to the school's upcoming pre-college exams, but there's no way she's giving them to the Joker until she gets the money and other tastes of "the good life" the Joker promised her. What might the Joker be planning?

In a plot twist somewhat progressive (perhaps unwittingly) for 1960s television, Susie's willing alliance with the Joker, not to mention her peer status with his adult henchmen, gives her a mature, self-reliant status beyond that of the other teens depicted more traditionally in the episode, including Dick Grayson. While it's unknown how Susie and the Joker initially crossed paths, it's clear that she has bought into the idea of crime being a faster and easier way toward the lavish living she demonstrably desires. Initially dazzled by the Joker's gifts of diamond-encrusted bracelets and fox stoles, and later luxuriating in the sensual sensations of these assumedly stolen baubles, Susie sashays with assuredness between her role as a high-schooler and that of a criminal accomplice plied with the spoils of the Joker's thievery. She even remarks that her landing a seat on the Woodrow Roosevelt High School Student Council merely allowed her the opportunity to flaunt her position of trust with adults to break rules and get whatever she wanted—including the exam answers sought by the Joker.

Susie's behavior also flirts with taboo, suggesting she might be open to a flirtatious or even physical relationship with the seemingly older men also connected to the Joker's criminal dealings. Nick makes clear overtures for her attention, which she strongly rebuffs, while the Joker sidles into her personal space at several opportune moments including a tight squeeze in the cab of a moving truck. Susie meets the Joker's advances with wide-eyed obliviousness—or perhaps responses calculated to entice his continued closeness? Either way, she continues to enjoy the tangible benefits of being on the villain's good side as he keeps the pricey prizes coming her way.

Such scandalous machinations between the two serve as a sort of precursor to a similarly shocking relationship depicted eighteen years later in issues of The *New Teen Titans* comics. Tara Markov, using her earth manipulation powers as the superhero Terra, joined the Teen Titans super-group as a full member and friend. Readers were surprised to learn that the fifteen-year-old Terra was not at all who she seemed, however, when it was revealed she had infiltrated the team to feed sensitive information to the super-villain assassin Deathstroke, who not only was her employer but also her lover despite being easily a generation older than her. The story arc known as "The Judas Contract" won the Comic Buyer's Guide Fan Award for Favorite Comic Book Story of 1984, and remains popular among comics readers today.

Compare Susie's characterization in these episodes to previous media depictions of wayward teen girls as being sweater-clad smokers and hangers-on to bad boys of the leather-jacket crowd. Girls in the outlaw biker movies of the 1950s as well as send-ups of such characters included in the beach party movies of the 1960s often exuded an aloof detachment from social norms. They were written with an assumption of being "fast and loose" young women, more ornamental possessions of the surrounding biker men than individuals interested in furthering themselves or profiting from any extralegal activities.

(Fun Bat Facts: Not only was Donna Loren, who played Susie in these episodes, also a featured performer in a number of beach party movies, but a member of Susie's cheerleading squad appeared as a "biker chick" in *Felony Squad*, a TV-movie that served as a pilot for an influential cop series. That chick-turned-cheerleader was Linda Harrison, who went on to play Nova in the first two *Planet of the Apes* films. *Felony Squad* starring Howard Duff and Dennis Cole, also ran on ABC during the same seasons as did *Batman*. It served as the inspiration for *Police Squad!*, the 1980s parody series and subsequent feature films starring Leslie Nielsen. We now return you to our regularly scheduled programming.)

Back in Gotham City and certain the Joker is up to something involving the school, Batman and Robin decide to stake out Woodrow Roosevelt High and wait for their nemesis to make his next move. Unbeknownst to the Dynamic Duo, Susie is already at the school! She warns the Joker, and with his help she prepares a trap for the crime fighters. Batman and Robin inspect the gym and find the gimmicked milk machine, but they're unable to avoid the trap it springs before knockout gas renders them unconscious.

Batman and Robin awaken to find themselves strapped to electric chairs inside a moving truck. The Joker takes great pleasure in having captured the Caped Crusaders, and draws their attention to the sinister slot machine mounted next to them. If the machine comes up with three Liberty Bells, Batman and Robin win their freedom and $50,000. Three oranges will give them their freedom with no money, but three lemons? 50,000 volts of electricity! The machine activates and the wheels start spinning, revealing two lemons before the episode ends. Holy cliffhanger!

"He Meets His Match, the Grisly Ghoul" picks up the action with the slot machine's final wheel spinning. They're saved by a timely blackout, as the entire city has fallen victim to the power failure that foils the Joker's devious plan. Along with the rest of the Bad Pennies gang, the Joker flees the scene before police arrive and rescue the trapped Batman and Robin.

Though Commissioner Gordon thinks there is no evidence

linking the Joker to this spate of criminal activity, Batman comes through with a secret tape recording he made. Analyzing the tape in the Batcave, the Dynamic Duo learns Susie is a member of the Joker's gang and armed with this information, they hatch their own daring plan: Robin, as Dick Grayson, will go undercover in an attempt to cozy up to Susie and infiltrate the Bad Pennies gang.

In an apparent nod to the adage that clothes make the man, we're treated here to an incognito Dick Grayson who appears more overwhelmed and way less confident as a would-be thug than he does when either himself in school and around stately Wayne Manor or in his crime-fighting best as Robin the Boy Wonder. Sporting shiny black leather in his oversized biker jacket and his spotless shoes, Dick—check that, "Dog George" as the undercover teen refers to himself in a two-way radio conversation with Batman—saunters into the Easy Living Candy Store and straight into the company of Susie and Nick.

Dick's strategy to glean info from the Bad Pennies crew is to cop an attitude that not only flies in the face of his own schoolyard reputation, but also his known connection as the ward of millionaire Bruce Wayne. He claims to have adopted the get-rich-quick criminal philosophy shared by the other Bad Pennies, calling his mentor a cheapskate who won't give Dick the money he needs for fun. Despite his provocative approaches to "Sue Baby" and his verbal dismissals of Nick, the Boy Wonder's handling of baddies is easier to see when he's in a cape and tights than when in biker garb. His hand is shown most clearly when he bobbles a cigarette, putting the wrong end of it in his mouth and then hastily correcting his mistake just before Nick lights the filter tip, and then brushes off a coughing fit by claiming already to have smoked two packs earlier in the day.

Again, the characterization of young troublemakers, indelibly seared into American pop culture in the form of such 1950s characters as Marlon Brando's Johnny Strabler in *The Wild One* and James Dean's Jim Stark in *Rebel Without a Cause*, had crept into cliché just a decade later. On television series of the era, many angsty, rebellious teens fell farther from threatening and more into the category of lovable irritant. Think beatnik Maynard G. Krebs in *The Many Loves of Dobie Gillis* and later Shaggy Jones on the *Scooby-Doo* cartoons, or wiseguy Eddie Haskell in *Leave It to Beaver*.

Within a year, an episode of *Dragnet* titled "The LSD Story" would push out the boundary of troubled youth stories. The story of Sergeant Joe Friday's encounter with the drug-addled Benjie the "Blue Boy" remains a milestone of television as the first example of established storytellers taking a hard swipe at the growing counterculture movement. Had this two-parter aired during the show's third season, might the Joker have been more inclined to lure teens into doing his criminal bidding not through greed but through the allure of psychedelic drugs? Likely not, but *Batman* did begin incorporating mod and hippie characters as well as more topical slang and counterculture elements in its later episodes.

Back at the candy shop and despite Dick's "best efforts" at acting the part of a petty criminal, henchman Nick has seen through the charade and arranges for Dick to be at the same bar robbed by Nick and Two-Bits to make a score of his own at precisely 3pm. Using this tip, Batman and Robin head for the bar, seemingly unaware they're walking into a trap as they await the appointed hour. As the clock strikes three, Robin inserts a coin into the jukebox and the shotgun appears again! Batman deploys a Batshield from his utility belt to protect them, before using a Batbomb to destroy the jukebox.

Realizing Susie's life is in danger from the Joker and the other Bad Pennies, Batman and Robin rush to the school where she's practicing with the cheerleaders in preparation for that night's basketball game between Woodrow Roosevelt High and Disko Tech. Talking with his bookie in Las Vegas, the Joker bets heavy for Disko Tech to win the game. If they win, he stands to rake in a million dollars? How can he be so confident?

It's the next part of his insidious plan! He's directed Susie to plant the stolen exam answers in the milk machine. Batman and Robin find her and try to warn her she's in danger, but she doesn't believe them. She tries some perfume given to her by the Joker, and falls unconscious. The perfume has been poisoned!

Believing Susie to be dead thanks to his perfume, the Joker and his henchmen return to Woodrow Roosevelt High. There, members of the basketball team standing at the gym's milk machine. They've found the exam answers! No sooner do they realize what's fallen into their laps than they're caught on camera by the Joker. Armed with this "obvious evidence" of the basketball team's apparent cheating, the Joker announces he will report the students so they'll be suspended and unable to play in the upcoming game, giving Disko Tech the win by default!

Not so fast! Batman and Robin have arrived in the nick of time, witnessing the entire sordid scene as it unfolds. Having saved Susie from the effects of the Joker's poison, the Caped Crusaders substituted the exam answers with fakes, keeping the students from seeing the real answers and endangering their college futures. The only thing left is to round up the Joker and his gang, which Batman and Robin do in their usual efficient manner (*Biff! Pow! Zap! Kapow! Whamm! Klonk!* And so on.)

Susie, remorseful for her part in the criminal plan, won't be sent to jail along with the Joker and his gang. Instead, she's being sent to the Wayne Foundation for Delinquent Girls. Dick promises to send her all new cheers so she can practice them and be ready for her return to school. Another caper is foiled, and another member of Batman's Rogues Gallery is once again behind bars!

The episode ends not only with the lead teens wistful and wiser but also with reestablishing Bruce Wayne, more so than even Batman, as the true hero of the two-parter. Both he and Dick recognize that Susie was a victim of circumstances as well as the Joker's machinations, with Dick attributing her straying from the straight and narrow to "an unhappy childhood and a broken home." Though she's understandably anxious about trading her flirtation with crime for a stint in a home for the wayward, she realizes that she's been given an opportunity for redemption. By stepping in and helping to redirect the course of Susie's life—a far cry from the fisticuffs and delivery to the Gotham City Jail he presumably bequeathed to the other Bad Pennies hoods—Wayne has done far more than simply rid the city of a potential felon. What he's done for Susie is consistent with what he's done at Wayne Manor: assembling the pieces of several broken families—the Graysons, the Coopers, the Waynes themselves—into a cohesive, functioning, repaired home.

In many ways and despite the lack of cape and cowl along with Batman's arsenal of crime fighting tools and skills, such actions are even more heroic than Wayne's exploits as the "World's Greatest Detective."

Dayton Ward is a *New York Times* bestselling author or co-author of nearly forty novels and novellas, often working with his best friend, Kevin Dilmore. His short fiction has appeared in more than 20 anthologies, and he's written for magazines such as *NCO Journal, Kansas City Voices, Famous Monsters of Filmland, Star Trek* and *Star Trek Communicator*, as well as the websites Tor.com, StarTrek.com, and Syfy.com. He lives in Kansas City with his wife and two daughters. Visit him on the web at http://www.daytonward.com.

Kevin Dilmore has teamed with author and best pal Dayton Ward for nearly twenty years on novels, shorter fiction and other writings chiefly in the Star Trek universe. As a senior writer for Hallmark Cards, Kevin has helped create books, Keepsake Ornaments, greeting cards and other products featuring characters from DC Comics, Marvel Comics, Star Trek, Star Wars, and other properties. He is a content approver for the recent Rainbow Brite comics series by Dynamite Entertainment. A contributor to publications including the Village Voice, *Amazing Stories, Star Trek Communicator*, and *Famous Monsters of Filmland*, he lives in Overland Park, Kansas.

ZOWIE!

True or False Take?

"True or False Face/Holy Rat Race"
By John S. Drew

Another glorious sun drenched day in Gotham City…

But as fans of *Batman* in 1966 would expect, as glorious as things appeared, they were quickly about to change. By the time those words, uttered by William Dozier, announcer and executive producer of the Batman series in the opening of "True or False Face", came over television sets across America, the series was a smash hit, credited as having saved the ABC Network. Legions of fans both young and old were tuning in each week and had already become accustomed to certain elements of the show, such as the cliffhanger, the Batfight, and Burt Ward's exclamations of "Holy" whatever.

Most important to this all was the opening segment of the first episode of any two-part story, which would introduce the villain of the week as he or she would set his or her evil scheme in motion. This, in turn, would lead to a moment of hand-wringing for Commissioner Gordon and Chief O'Hara before they would pick up the hotline to the Dynamic Duo. It was even more important in this particular episode as the producers introduced a new villain to what some now call the "Dozierverse", so named after Batman producer William Dozier.

But how new was False Face?

Turn back the clock to February 1958, issue #113 of DC Comics' *Batman*. "The Menace of False Face" is a very brief story, all of eight pages, at the start of the issue. In this comic, False Face has a specific method of operation in that he always manages to detain the person he will impersonate in order to get away with his theft. It's enough to cause a brief problem for Batman who manages to capture False Face and his gang by tricking the gang into thinking *he* is False Face.

Many argue this is the same False Face episode writer Stephen Kandel would introduce eight years later in the TV show. It is possible, but there is also enough in this story to suggest that simply the name and the gimmick of quick change are all that are taken from that issue of Batman. Considering the character only appears once in the comic and is never named, it is possible that Kandel simply read the story and thought the concept intriguing enough to develop into a two-parter for the first season of the TV series.

If you take the character of False Face in the series as he is presented, there is something more to him than we see in the comic book. Like many of the villains in the television series, he has an inclination towards leaving clues that will tip the Dynamic Duo off to his next crime. His clues take the form of sentences with wording that has the exact opposite meaning. It's how the Dynamic Duo is able to deduce that False Face plans to rob the Aladdin Armored Company.

In the comic, False Face, when not in disguise, wears a black mask over his eyes and nose, leaving his mouth and chin visible. In the television series, his entire face is covered by a cloudy plastic mask that manages to obscure his features just enough to be unnerving as you watch him snarl from the small opening in the mouth of his mask.

And then there is the matter of his assistants. In the comic, False Face works with his henchmen, a group of suit wearing gangsters. In the TV show, he has three goons, dressed in robber outfits from the 1940s, complete with domino masks. Like many of the goons in the first season of the series, they are more than just something for Batman and Robin to punch. They have individual names, and even more important to False Face's scheme, they have their own skill-sets which he employs in his plot.

There is also the added bonus of the beautiful Blaze who comes across as more than just the usual moll in this story. In most episodes of Batman, the role of the moll is to look pretty, ask the questions to prompt the villain to reveal his or her plan to the audience, and to, in many cases, succumb to Batman's charm and discover the right path in life. Blaze fit all these requirements, but there was something more to her. She wasn't an assistant. She was a partner.

The story opens with Blaze and False Face entering the jewelry store where the Mergenberg Crown is on display at the Gotham City Exhibit Hall. It is Blaze who stands in the foreground and speaks, as the Princess Mergenberg, while False Face stands in the background. Indeed, one can argue this is more a Blaze episode than it is a False Face one. He doesn't come to the forefront as a character until the second half, and even then he spends most of it in one disguise or other.

And what did this mean to the actor portraying False Face?

There are many stories that are told about this episode. To wit: Actor Malachi Throne requested his name be taken off the usual "Guest Villain" title card as he discovered he was getting paid less than his co-star, Myrna Fahey, who played Blaze. The reason the character didn't return to the show for a second bout with Batman was that the mask used to hide Throne's features was too grotesque, making him look like a burn victim. The identity of False Face was a closely guarded secret with many speculating it was Frank Sinatra or Dean Martin who posed under the mask. While many of these stories have been confirmed by the cast and crew of the series, it is interesting to note that some of them can be debunked by a simple scan of newspaper reports of the time.

To put things in some perspective, "True or False Face", the first of the two-part story, aired on March 9, 1966. There were mentions of the character of False Face as early as the day before the January premiere of the series in the papers as producer Dozier touted the new villains that would appear alongside well-known ones such as the Penguin and the Joker. By early February though the cat was out of the bag and the syndicated TV Scout column was reporting that actor Malachi Throne would portray False Face.

Who?

That was the question many were asking, as the man playing False Face appeared to be as much a mystery as his character.

Malachi Throne began his acting career as a theatrical player, and a peer to greats like Marlon Brando. His career was sidetracked by a call to army service in the Korean War. When he returned, he continued in the theater, but also began to make appearances on various television shows. From 1959-1966 he appeared in twenty-five television shows in a variety of roles. While he was magnificent in each, he never got the recognition or the steady work his acting abilities should have received. Indeed, his longest stint on television in a recurring role was six episodes of *Ben Casey* as Martin Phelps.

So it stood to reason that many would question who the man behind the mask was in the two-part *Batman* episode, but in fact, the mystery behind the actor actually lent credibility to the mystery of the character itself. Throne had a deep, resonant voice that worked well with the classical Greek style mask that adorned his face. He compensated for not being able to work his features into his performance by making grand gestures with his hands to punctuate words, and high jumps and kicks of delight when his plan was working his way. The single sequence in the episode where you get an idea of what Throne looks like, as the armored car driver, is muted though as he wears a prosthetic nose and then talks through it as the scene plays out.

The mystery behind the villain plays into a scheme of flooding the city with counterfeit money. This seems like an obvious choice of crimes considering his moniker, but there are some nice touches in the episode that also reveal falsehoods one may not discover without closer inspection.

For instance, the deathtrap in "True or False Face", another customary element of the first and second season that would end the first episode and entice the viewer to return the following night to see the resolution, seems simple enough at first glance: Batman and Robin are tied to a subway track as a train is barreling towards them. However, Robin is tied to the track going in the opposite direction. It is only really Batman who appears to be in danger as the episode draws to a close. However, there is a great horrific element to this trap that is overlooked due to its seeming simplicity—Robin will witness Batman die in horrifying agony before it is his turn with a train that will eventually approach from the other direction.

It is only through an ad placed on the radio that Alfred hears while cleaning the Batcave that the two are able to escape. That ad leads to another falsehood or deception that still intrigues me every time I watch this story. Batman and Robin decide to determine who sent the ad with the cryptic message, "Many are called, but two are chosen," to the station. There, they meet with station manager Leo Gore, played by character actor Michael Fox. Yes, *the* Michael Fox, the man who caused later performer Michael J. Fox to add the "J" to his stage name.

When you look at this one scene he plays opposite the Dynamic Duo, you would think for a moment that he is False Face. He is about the same height as the character and has the same tonality, if not as deep, as Malachi Throne. It's a nice bit of casting and misdirection on the producers' part, although quite possibly not the intention of writer Stephen Kandel. One other piece of trivia regarding Fox: He appeared in the first two episodes of the season as Inspector Basch, a character many thought would be recurring. The thick glasses he wears as Leo Gore obscure his face enough that you might miss it—another falsehood.

There is also the falsehood of Blaze, both the character and the actress who portrays her. As the story opens, she is set up as False Face's equal. She is capable of guise and guile on par with the "Master of Devilish Disguise." It is only Batman who sees through her disguise of an older messenger in Gordon's office and yet she is prepared to escape, surprising everyone as she leaps out Gordon's thirteenth-floor window. Throughout the episode she wears a constant assortment of colorful wigs, and is striking in every in which but we don't know what she really looks like. We get a glimpse of her in Part One as False Face reveals the hidden crown under one of her wigs, but it isn't until the final scene as she prepares to leave for New Zealand to work the farm with her humble, but honest brother that we see her as she truly is—a brunette.

And not just any brunette. Many at the time compared actress Myrna Fahey to Elizabeth Taylor and you can clearly see the comparison to be a fair one. It helped land her the role Taylor played in *Father of the Bride*, Katherine Banks, when the movie was adapted for television in 1961. It is curious though how she managed to score a higher pay for her time on *Batman* compared to Malachi Throne, since Throne was working much more steadily than she was at the time. In fact, she would only make six more television appearances before her death in 1973.

Perhaps it was the fact that Throne wasn't actually clocking as much screen-time in the two-part episode as False Face would disguise himself as Chief O'Hara, Commissioner Gordon, a bank guard, and a cowboy in the story. In fact, False Face remained as O'Hara through most of the final third of "True or False Face."

Or perhaps it was the fact that Fahey was known enough to the *Batman* producers through her work on *Father of the Bride*, a show she tried to get out of towards the end of its run as she felt the focus was more on the father and not on the bride. The producers were well established for bringing in talent that at the time you might not think of when it came to Batman. For example, many questioned the producers' judgment in bringing in Cesar Romero for the role of the Joker. And yet, even with his mustache intact, he is for many Ground Zero when approaching the character to portray on screen.

A similar thought process may have been engaged in bringing Fahey to the *Batman* series.

Finally, there is the falsehood of False Face's hideout, Bioscope Studios. The movie production company is false, having been created for the show but the fact that False Face hides in the shadows of an establishment formerly known for creating its own reality is also appropriate.

It also adds to the already cinematic feel to this story. While pretty much all of the first season is shot in a way that you could easily see playing in a movie theater, an effect that makes for a smooth transition to the theatrical release of the *Batman* feature film in the summer of 1966, this episode stands out among the others for its extensive use of exterior shooting.

William A. Graham gets only one turn at bat as a director on this series, just as the villain of this piece does, but his work stands out as well as the character he is directing. From the nicely choreographed fight scene in the small confines of a bank vault to the dizzying chase of False Face's chameleon-like truck through the streets of Gotham and the ruins of Bioscope Pictures, Graham presents a smooth-moving story that never lags.

The music that accompanies the story works as well. There is a mischievous playfulness to the False Face theme developed by Nelson Riddle that is punctuated by the frenetic movements of Throne himself. It's a shame the music is never used in another False Face story, but it is repurposed for future second season episodes.

The supporting cast, except for Aunt Harriet, is used to good effect as well. Stafford Repp as Chief O'Hara and Neil Hamilton as Commissioner Gordon get to play False Face impersonating each respectively and do a good turn with the struggles the disguise artist would have in making the quick changes he does. Alan Napier is always a joy to watch in any episode of *Batman* and he gets his moment as he saves the Dynamic Duo from doomsday-by-train.

Sadly, Madge Blake is given short shrift here as she appears only at the start of the story as Bruce and Dick once again go off to answer the call to duty, this time with an explanation of taking a "ramble in the woods," or as they say, "nature in the raw, so to speak." This was a clear thumbing of the show's collective nose at critic Fredric Wertham, the infamous psychiatrist who a decade earlier questioned the sexuality of a man living alone with a young male ward.

As it is the first season, both Adam West and Burt Ward continue to be in top form as the Caped Crusaders with the latter belting out every "Holy" exclamation with unbridled zest and the former delivering his lines with incredibly believable sincerity. A special tip of the cowl must be given to West as you can hear some congestion in his delivery of lines in this story. The actor was recovering from the flu during filming of the False Face episode which had landed him in the hospital for five days.

As a screenwriter, Stephen Kandel's stories are usually hit or miss, in my opinion. He has contributed some of the most memorable stories to television series such as *Star Trek* (with the creation of the character Harry Mudd), *Wonder Woman*, and *The Wild, Wild West*. At the same time, he has failed to bring out the inherent wonder of such shows as *The Six Million Dollar Man*.

With False Face, he has managed to write a serviceable enough story that is neither good nor bad. Overall it works, despite having some plot holes that leave you wondering. For example, why steal the crown in the first place? Why was the gimmick of using false quotes used only once, but was clearly noted at the start of the story? When robbing the vault, where was the counterfeit money that False Face was going to replace the good money with?

What elevates this story is Throne's performance as False Face, one that stands out despite the mask and limited screen time. For me, it is why when I finish watching the episode I want to see more and am disappointed that the producers never went back to this singular villain again.

In retrospect, the reasoning that the mask was grotesque may have been true, but considering other villains were given costume changes (and facial changes in the form of different actors playing the roles) in subsequent appearances, how difficult would it have been to develop a different False Face visage to keep the mystery going in a second or third season story? It is a truly sad aspect to what is a mostly wonderful story that is extremely re-watchable.

And that leads to the final falsehood of the story.

As False Face is led away at story's end, he tells Batman, "You may yet meet your match." One could look at that as a threat to Batman for the villain's return or perhaps a warning that some clever criminal will beat the Caped Crusader one day. If the former, it's a shame we don't get a follow-through on the threat, but if it's the latter, we know that there are many more thrilling adventures of Batman and Robin to come in the series.

John S. Drew has been a writer, educator, doorman, librarian, father, podcaster, and hostage negotiator in his more than half-century on this Earth. His writings include fiction in the *Star Trek*, *Spider-Man*, *Lost in Space* and *Doctor Who* universes. His podcasting is nostalgic/pop culture-driven with shows focused on *Batman*, *Doctor Who*, *The Six Million Dollar Man*, *The Bionic Woman*, *Shazam*, *The Secrets of Isis*, *The Super Friends*, and more. He lives in New York with his wife, two teens, and a menagerie of pets that could earn him an ark in the next great flood.

ZOK!

Propinquity Killed the Cat

"The Purr-fect Crime/Better Luck Next Time"
By Mark Racop

I saw my first episode in its original run when I was two years old, and I am honored and thrilled to write a review of my favorite pair of episodes from the show—and from a Batmobile-centric point of view. Why Batmobile-centric, you might be wondering? My company is Fiberglass Freaks, the only licensed builder of the 1966 Batmobile replicas in the world. We sell three models of cars ranging from the modest to the magnificent. Our top-of-the-line car is an almost exact duplicate of the #1 car used on the TV show, but with one difference—all of the gadgets are *real* on our cars!

As a huge 1966 Batmobile fan (and archivist), there are three go-to episodes in which to really check out the car. The first is the pilot, "Hi Diddle Riddle/Smack in the Middle," where we see the Batscope, the Bat-O-Stat Anti-Fire Activator, the Remote Batcomputer, and the Detect-a-scope all first used; the second is "The Purr-fect Crime/Better Luck Next Time," where we see the Batometer, Batbeam, Bat Armor, and the Automatic Tire Repair Device used; and the third is "Clock King's Crazy Crimes/The Clock King Gets Crowned," where we see the Batscope and Batphotoscope used. My favorite of these is the first Catwoman two-parter. In addition to being a fantastic two-part episode, there are some really neat shots of the car, there were several Batmobile batgadgets introduced, and there were several features that were used only in it.

Did you have the GAF View-Master Batman set when you were a kid? I couldn't tell you how many times I watched and rewatched the View-Master set of "The Purr-fect Crime." I bought two more mint sets as an adult, but still have my original, complete with the beat-up sleeve, the beat-up storybook, and the original three reels. What was it about this episode that stood out so much? Why did I enjoy it enough to call it my favorite of the entire series?

"The Purr-fect Crime/Better Luck Next Time" was the *perfect Batman* episodes (with "True or False Face/Holy Rat Race" a close second). Unlike the formulaic episodes that plagued much of the show later, "Purr-fect" really stood out. Catwoman was a formidable opponent for Batman. This wouldn't be shocking for a new movie in today's environment, but in the 1960s, this was some feat. She was intelligent, tall, sexy, confident, and most of all...she was dangerous. Just like the Catwoman herself, the path for the story was mysterious and unpredictable, too. Even after seeing this show at least one hundred times, I find myself drawn into it again and again, making it tough to analyze.

If you haven't bought the Blu-ray version of the TV series, you owe it to yourself to do whatever it takes to make it happen. They went to the original negatives and created an absolutely beautiful print. The color and clarity are so vivid. And nowhere but in the first season do you find the *Batman* filmmakers doing a more magnificent job using that unique, signature color and lighting. Howard Schwartz was the director of photography for these episodes (He won two Emmys and was nominated for six more). While watching them, it's easy to see why. I like how dark and moody the lighting was in "Purr-fect." The use of shadows was incredibly effective, yet in a perfect juxtaposition we see the primary colors of Batman and Robin's costumes were well-lit. There were many unique camera angle decisions, like an over-the-shoulder shot in Gordon's office that had never been done before (or since).

The episode begins with Catwoman dispatching a guard and stealing a golden cat statue. Then Bonnie, Commissioner Gordon's secretary, delivered a live kitten with a newspaper clipping on the collar to Gordon and O'Hara (this was the one and only time we actually *saw* Bonnie on-screen, by the way). The clipping was of Mark Andrews, the owner of the stolen cat statue, indicating that he had a matching cat statue at the Gotham City Exposition. Gordon and O'Hara were allowed to be competent in the first season; they deduced that Catwoman was the perpetrator of the crime. Then, Gordon made the Hotline call.

Alfred interrupted Bruce and Dick playing four-dimensional chess, much to Dick's delight—he would rather stick to Latin crossword puzzles than have to think fourteen moves ahead. Alfred gave one of the more lame excuses as to why the two must leave Aunt Harriet, but it sufficed. Bruce and Dick quickly answered Gordon's call, and jumped to the Batpoles.

Per normal, we cut to the animated titles next. Have you ever wondered what that weird red and white "spinning thing" was that started the titles? It's a still of the Start Button label on the dashboard, along with a red and white button, spun quickly. Pause and go frame by frame on it the next time you watch any episode.

We came back from the commercial break to see Batman and Robin rushing to the Batmobile. The car was a modified 1955 Lincoln Futura, though many thought it was a GTO, a Cadillac, Chrysler, or any car with big fins, but it was indeed the Lincoln Futura concept car used in the 1959 movie *It Started With a Kiss*, starring Debbie Reynolds and Glenn Ford.

Originally, Dean Jeffries (builder of the Monkeemobile and the Black Beauty) was supposed to modify a 1959 Cadillac into Batman's ride, but when ABC pushed *Batman* forward by half a year to be a mid-season replacement, there was no way that Jeffries could complete the task in time. The producers turned to customizer George Barris, who had access to the Futura. He extended the fins onto the doors, extended the hood scoop to the nose of the car, opened up the wheel wells, and scalloped the fins. A gloss black paint job was topped off with neon red/orange striping called "fluorescent cerise" that Barris says he bought at a sign shop.

Barris bought the car from Ford Motor Company for just one dollar. He sold the car at Barrett-Jackson on January 19th, 2013 for $4.2 million ($4.62 million after auction fees), the highest price ever paid for a movie or TV car. Holy great investment!

Even today, I still feel the excitement that I did as a two-year-old, watching the Dynamic Duo jump in the car, discuss the atomic batteries and the turbines, see the flame shooting out the back, and watch them rocket out of the cave. My heart still races as I see them drive over the folding barricade and make the hairpin turn towards Gotham City, some fourteen miles away.

A side note: Batman's driving was considered so poor on the show (crossing the center line, speeding, not using his turn signals, and not fastening his seat belt) that the show drew a scathing letter from the National Safety Council, calling Batman "the world's worst driver." The 1955 Lincoln Futura did not have seatbelts, so this Catwoman episode was made to answer to that complaint. Safety Bat-Belts were quickly added—pink with a black stripe—and black bats on red squares were applied to its airplane-styled buckles.

Back in the episode, our heroes headed to Police Headquarters, where Batman agreed that the golden cat statue was but the first of many cat-related crimes to come from Catwoman. A quick meeting with Mark Andrews revealed that the other cat statue was at the Gotham Exposition, and the exhibit ended that day.

Just outside of police headquarters, Batman clearly fastened his seatbelt (across his rib cage, not waist) and pressed the ignition button in roll-top dash compartment #2, but heard an alarm. He turned to Robin to say, "Robin, you haven't fastened your Safety Bat-Belt."

"We're only going a couple of blocks," the Boy Wonder replied.

Batman lectured his youthful ward, "It won't be long until you're old enough to get a driver's license, Robin. And then you'll be able to drive the Batmobile and other vehicles. Remember, motorist safety."

Robin fastened his belt and said, "Gosh Batman, when you put it that way..."

A side note to the side note: My parents were divorced when I was young. Without a father figure in the home every single day, Adam West's Batman became my father figure when I wasn't with my dad. I took the life lessons that Adam's Batman taught Robin very seriously. Imagine my surprise when I saw my dad fastening his seatbelt...wow, my dad takes Batman seriously, too, thought! He even fastens his seat belt!

We then cut to Catwoman's hideout at the Gato & Chat Wholesale Fur Retail Co., where we saw Catwoman's spectacular entrance. Seen only in shadow at first, it wasn't until she turned on the light to reveal the Princess of Plunder that we witnessed the beautiful Julie Newmar in that exquisitely tailored Lurex costume. This was her only appearance in the first season; she appeared half a dozen times in the second season. Interestingly, Newmar was the first person to ever play the role of Catwoman for film or television. Lee Meriwether played Catwoman in the 1966 movie (while Newmar had a back injury and was shooting the film *Mackenna's Gold*), and then Eartha Kitt took over the role in the third season.

Since the 1966 *Batman* TV series, Catwoman has been played in live-action by Michelle Pfeiffer, Halle Berry, Anne Hathaway, Maggie Baird, and Camren Bicondova, and voiced by Adrienne Barbeau, Eliza Dushku, and Gina Gershon for the animated versions.

Leo, a henchmen played by former Tarzan actor Jock Mahoney, gave Catwoman the multi-volume *History of Gotham City*, while the scaredy-cat henchman Felix, perfectly played by Ralph Manza, confirmed the delivery of the kitten to Commissioner Gordon. Catwoman laughed greedily as she studied the story of the lost treasure of Captain Manx, a pirate from Gotham City's early days.

Back at the Batcave, we saw some things about the Batmobile

that were unique to this episode. Batman said to Alfred, "While the atomic reactor is recharging the Batmobile, please help Robin with the Auxiliary Power Channel. Time is of the essence."

So Alfred helped Robin hold a clear plastic tube, inserted *into* the flame-throwing rocket exhaust tube and issuing yellow smoke into it! Some of the smoke escaped the end of the tube, and the show editor *had* to cut to Batman, who asked the two to "increase the power to seventeen triple O KW (17,000 kilowatts for the rest of us). Once that level was reached, Batman called for "all power off."

One of the things I always appreciated about the 1966 Batman is that he was genuinely smart. Unlike the movie Batmans, Adam's Caped Crusader was brilliant at everything he did, and earned the nickname of "The World's Greatest Detective." He used chemistry, computers, logic, history, grammar, and a vast amount of knowledge on every topic to deduce the criminal activity of the show's villains. This episode in particular was one of the finest examples of using his knowledge about radioactivity and chemistry to his advantage. This version of Batman stepped right off the comic book page.

In keeping with the camp nature of the show, though, Batman hilariously put rubber gloves *over* his blue satin gloves before he went to work. He told Alfred that the plan was to treat the cat statue with a tiny mist of a non-deadly form of radioactivity so they could trace it within a fifty-mile radius. The Caped Crusaders then sped out of the Batcave in the Batmobile.

The ticket taker at the Exposition was none other than Leo, in disguise. He tried to let Batman and Robin into the hall for free, but Batman insisted on paying "just like any normal citizen."

In the Exhibition hall, the Caped Crusaders treated the cat statue with the radioactive spray. At almost midnight, Batman left Robin to check the rest of the exposition, promising to return in an oddly specific "three minutes and twenty seconds."

Catwoman entered through a sarcophagus and used her cat to attack Robin. The Boy Wonder barely managed to message Batman with his Bat Communicator before he fell unconscious. I really enjoyed Catwoman's dialogue when she saw Batman for the first time in this episode: "Is that any way to greet an old friend, Batman? Not even a hello, how are you? Teach him some manners, fellows!"

Batman fought Catwoman's henchmen until he saw Robin's unconscious form, and Catwoman, Felix, and Leo escaped with the golden cat. This was the Sixties, and the feeling then was that there would someday be a pill to cure everything. Batman was no different, and even had a "universal drug antidote pill" to revive Robin after Catwoman drugged him with Catacol.

Batman and Robin used the Batometer in the Batmobile roll-top dash door #3 to track the stolen cat to Catwoman's lair. Clearly seen on the surface of the closed dash door #5 was the "Tire Repair Device" label that was used later in the story. This was also the first appearance of the Batram lever. Located on the dash top, we can clearly see the Batram and the "Batram" label in the close-up shots, but they were not in any of the wide-angle shots in these episodes. The Batram will later be employed in "A Riddle A Day Keeps the Riddler Away/When the Cat's Away the Mice Will Play." Perhaps even more curiously, the "Detect-a-scope" label was now *under the arch*, in front of the five light sequence flasher, instead of on the radar-like device on Robin's dash top.

The Dynamic Duo used the Batometer to trace the radioactive residue to the Gato & Chat Fur Wholesalers warehouse. The production value on this episode was high as they did more night shooting in the first season. The moody lighting was perfect as the Batmobile pulled into the alley, near the ever-present blue Dodge A100 villain van.

Robin recognized the words *gato* and *chat* as Spanish and French respectively for the word "cat." Batman expressed his admiration for Robin's expertise of foreign languages, "which come in handy in fighting crime." Robin replied, "*Si, si*, Batman."

Batman then said, "There are no entrances and only one door. We have no choice. We'll use the Batbeam in the Batmobile."

Robin replied, "Why don't we just walk right in?"

Batman countered, "Because the door may be booby trapped. We won't take any chances if we use the Batbeam."

They raised the Batbeam using the increase-output knob on the dashtop. The color of the Batbeam antenna had changed from silver to gold/brass. All four masts of the antenna were functional, unlike later episodes where it came up only halfway, or couldn't fully retract. Batman fired the Batbeam at the door and there was a small explosion at the handle.

Robin said, "You're right again, Batman. We might've been killed."

And, as could only be said by the late, great Adam West, Batman added "Or worse."

They entered the warehouse, only to fall through a trap door. Catwoman was expecting them, of course. Her character was so well-written, and Julie Newmar did such a great job of personifying the role. Catwoman always seemed a step ahead of Batman. She teased him, saying things like, "How does it feel to be the quarry for a change?" and "Why don't you just admit that I'm smarter than you." This characterization was in stark contrast to the love-sick Catwoman of later episodes, who didn't know what the word propinquity was!

She toyed with the Caped Crusaders with spiked walls closing in on them. Batman tried to hold the walls apart with brute strength, but discovered that the spikes were just rubber. Next up, another prank: Felix left a bomb through a cat door, but the explosion was harmless. Batman picked up the bomb and was startled when a cat's screech accompanied a flag that popped out. Appropriately, the word "Meow!" was on the flag.

Then the real drama began. A descending tube encircled Robin and drew him up from the room. The spiked walls pulled away, and Catwoman gave Batman a choice between two doors: a tiger was behind one, and she was behind the other. He chose the wrong door, and the "Batman-eating tiger" sprang into action! To find out if Batman would ever see Robin alive again, or if Robin would ever see Batman alive again, we had to tune in tomorrow night, "same Cat Time; same Cat Channel!"

The Batman stunt-double working with the tiger looked pretty convincing, until you noticed his white mustache. Thankfully the clever editing, the lighting, and the angle of his head kept us from noticing too many times.

Batman fended off the tiger long enough to pull out Batclaws from his utility belt and climb a wall. And then, in perfect 1966 Batman absurdity, he wore Batearplugs on the *outside* of his cowl, so when he reversed the polarity on the communicator in his belt buckle the sound wouldn't affect him. The right ear plug was missing in a few shots, but mysteriously reappeared later. The sonic wave caused the tiger to lie down, and Batman exited through the very door the tiger came through and slid it closed behind him.

Catwoman poured catnip on Robin, then had Felix and Leo use a teeter-totter setup with sand to lower the Boy Wonder into a pit full of tigers. Robin's greatest line in this episode had to be when he said, "Catwoman, you are *not* a nice person!" I loved Julie's exit as she spun around to meow, right before heading out the door.

Luckily Batman found Robin in time to save him, using a Batarang and Batrope to swing in to his rescue. One of the more brutal fight scenes ensued, with chains, torches, and tigers involved. The Dynamic Duo won, of course, but Leo managed to escape. He met up with Catwoman, who was not pleased that Batman and Robin were still alive, that Felix was captured, and that Leo left the cat statues behind. Catwoman accurately deduced that Batman would discover their secret, and put "alternate plan B" into effect.

In the Batcave, an examination of the statues revealed that the two cats had different markings on their backs. This was odd, because they were supposed to be identical. Batman read up on the Captain Manx story, and learned that the pirate's treasure chest that the pirate was going to give the city was never recovered. Batman held the cats together, and found that they formed a treasure map leading right to the treasure.

Robin wondered if they could track Catwoman if she had been exposed to the radioactive mist long enough. The Boy Wonder *manually* opened the trunk of the Batmobile to put the cats in the lead-lined compartment, then dropped the trunk lid with a loud *kabang*!

In a later Catwoman episode ("Hi Diddle Diddle/The Cat and the Fiddle"), the trunk raised and lowered automatically. The Batometer indicated Catwoman's location, but Batman said that they had better put on the Batmobile's Batarmor because Catwoman knew that they're coming. Even still, then they don't do anything different with the car!

Catwoman mined the road. The Batmobile survived, thanks to the aforementioned-but-not-installed Batarmor, but the tires went flat. Robin activated the tire repair device, which was located on the *outside* of the fourth roll-top dashboard door. The tires automatically re-inflated.

Let me take a moment to talk about the dashboard labels in the Batmobile. These labels were continuously changed throughout the series. Over time and in different episodes, the left red and white dash button was the Bat Ray Projector, Batbeam Firing Button, and even the Detect-a-scope! The increase-output knob on the dashboard was labeled Homing Receiver Scope, Radar Scope, Antenna Activator, Police Band Cut-In Switch, and Detect-a-scope. The blue triangle knobs on the center console were never labeled or used, and the same goes for the silver Ansen T-handle lever on the center console.

Inside a cave, Catwoman found the Captain Manx treasure, but her greed prevented her from sharing with Leo and cnce he filled the loot bag, she gassed him. She led Batman and Robin on a merry chase through the cave, which was a decent set...except for the shaking stalactite (Look closely on the View-Master reels and you'll catch a glimpse of the top of the set's cave backdrop). She tried to jump across a chasm, but was too weighed down by her loot. Unwilling to let go of her treasure so Batman could save her, Catwoman fell into the unknown depths below. The Dynamic Duo finds only her cat.

In the "tag" scene back at stately Wayne Manor, Alfred gave Dick advice for another four-level chess game, but Bruce won anyway. Aunt Harriet entered, frustrated by Catwoman's cat, who stole the lobster.

When "The Purr-fect Crime" originally aired, the broadcast was interrupted by news about NASA astronauts Neil Armstrong and David Scott. They were in real trouble on Gemini 8 and were almost killed. ABC was flooded with calls, but the calls weren't from listeners concerned about Armstrong and Scott—they were upset that *Batman* was interrupted. Holy Wrong Priorities!

In conclusion, I really think "The Purr-fect Crime/Better Luck Next Time" was a purr-fect mix of action-adventure, camp, and a hint of film-noir. The writing, directing, and acting were top-notch, and the production value was outstanding. It was the 1966 *Batman* TV show at its best.

As a lifelong 1966 Batman fan, **Mark Racop** has wanted to own the Batmobile since he was two-years-old. At the age of seventeen, he made it happen, building his first 1966 Batmobile replica from a 1974 Monte Carlo. Now, he and his Fiberglass Freaks build 1966 Batmobile replicas for a living in Logansport, Indiana. Racop's replicas are full-scale, drivable cars that have sold all over the world. As of the publishing date, he has completed twenty-eight replicas during his sixteen years in business. In 2010, D.C. Comics and Warner Brothers licensed Fiberglass Freaks to build them as officially licensed products. Racop is frequently a guest speaker at conventions, clubs, and at high schools and colleges across the mid-West.

ZLONK!

The Finest Feathered Forty-Six Minutes

"The Penguin Goes Straight/Not Yet, He Ain't"
By Joe Crowe

The Penguin debuted in *Detective Comics* #58 in 1941, but Burgess Meredith brought him to squawking, sophisticated life in *Batman*. Since then, every creator of every Penguin story has been chasing the best story with Penguin in it, the *Batman* episode "The Penguin Goes Straight" and "Not Yet, He Ain't." which aired March 23 and 24 in 1966.

I will forgive the title of the second part of the episode for the usually unforgivable crime of spoiling the whole story. It's that good.

Batman has the best rogue's gallery, but Penguin gets crowded out of the top of anyone's favorites list by Cesar Romero's Joker, Frank Gorshin's Riddler, and all the Catwomans. I stake a claim on Penguin as my favorite, and this episode contains the reasons why.

The whole episode is based around a villainous plan that I had never seen before outside of pro wrestling: the bad guy turned good.

Of course—as the title of the second half spoils—he didn't really make the switch, but that was the first time I had encountered such a storyline. Granted, I saw the episode when I was somewhat young and maybe not super well-read. But my point is this episode took a rare path to get to the usual end result of Batman and Robin punching dudes.

These episodes show that Penguin is a genius. When I originally watched this episode, the two parts were out of order and I watched whenever they were on. I've now discovered that this episode is only Penguin's second appearance on *Batman*.

So he went to this crazy switcheroo plan on only his second time out in the field.

Here are more reasons why Penguin is my favorite:

He's called the Penguin, yet does not wear a bird costume. He has no bird-related powers. The Riddler leaves nothing to the imagination; his gimmick is right there on his costume, just like with Catwoman. Mr. Freeze tells you his whole deal right there in his name.

But the Penguin? None of that is sophisticated enough. He believes that crime requires formal wear that would be acceptable in high society. Dress for the job you want.

He wears a tuxedo, yet most ornithologists agree that penguins do not wear tuxedos. That's their actual skin, they claim. Penguin's primary offensive weapon is an umbrella. Few would argue that penguins can use umbrellas, for the generally accepted science is that they have no opposable thumbs whereby they could manipulate an umbrella.

What does wearing a tuxedo and wielding an umbrella have to do with penguins? *No one knows.*

Why a penguin? There are lots of other fearsome avian creatures that would strike terror into the hearts of Gotham's citizens. Why is he a penguin? *No one knows.*

The only penguin-ish thing he does is waddle, sometimes. The squawk in his speech must surely speak to his 1960s-era sophistication. He clearly does not want to remove the fancy cigarette holder from his mouth. I mean, what is smoking going to do, kill him?

I must applaud Penguin's choice of headquarters in these episodes. The Penguin does not mess around with fourth-rate hideouts like warehouses. Even basements are beneath him (I shan't apologize for that pun. I've been watching the show a lot).

Other parts of the story are really good, too, and by that I mean, totally nut-bonkers crazy. I also mean it in comparison to other episodes of this show, so the bar is already set pretty high on the "wonderfully nuts" scale.

When the episode begins, the voiceover guy says it's "a beautiful Wednesday afternoon in Gotham City." While he says that, the Gotham skies are gray and citizens are shown bundled up to avoid the cold.

When Penguin foils an armed robbery thanks to his umbrella skills, Commissioner Gordon has no freaking idea what's going on and calls in Batman and Robin, leading to a solid comedy gold moment.

He calls on the Bat-phone and Alfred answers, but at that moment, Messrs. Bruce and Dick are enjoying some costume-free time with Aunt Harriet.

Let me rephrase that: They're enjoying some time out of their Bat-costumes with Aunt Harriet.

Let me rephrase that again: They're enjoying some time in their civilian guises with Aunt Harriet.

Alfred gloriously reveals that he has a code for when a Bat-call comes in and Aunt Harriet is in the same room. "Telephone call for you, sir. It's a Mr. Rime. Mr. K. Rime."

While Batman and Robin make their way to police headquarters, Batman suggests to the commish that he and Chief O'Hara rough up a captured bad guy for information. Specifically they say, "Give that crook a grilling."

My friend and fellow Bat-connoisseur Geena Phillips said this about the interrogation scene (and better than I could): "I can scarcely think of anything more adorable and less menacing than being interrogated by Commissioner Gordon and Chief O'Hara.

Seriously, the chief has never more closely resembled the Maytag Repairman then he does in this scene. I really don't want to sully this interrogation scene by describing it too much, because it is a comedy freaking masterpiece."

Penguin lays out his plan to his henchmen, which is a nice change from spilling his guts to Batman and Robin while they have time to escape whichever trap he's put them in. The goons aren't really into the plan, because, as they rightly point out, they are still likely to get Bat-mudholes stomped into them.

Alfred again shows that he is the most valuable player of this episode as he goes undercover to get Penguin to reveal that he has not reformed. Here is Batman's plan: Steal an heiress' jewels. Replace them with fake jewels that contain a Bat-tracking gizmo. Batman and Robin are advocating and abetting grand theft.

Gotham hosts a gala to benefit his new security service, which shows Gotham citizens to be remarkably interested in immediate forgiveness.

Penguin's plan is going really great. Gotham loves him and is irate at the thieving Dynamic Duo. So naturally, he decides to chuck the whole thing and just kill Batman and Robin.

First he knocks the fudge out of the duo with an umbrella filled with cement. Why Penguin refrained from using this same weapon during every future caper is beyond me, but I bet it would go something like this:

Robin: Holy bumbershoot, Penguin's got the concrete umbrella again!

Concrete umbrella: KLONK.

Announcer: Will Robin recover from serious head trauma in time? Stay tuned tomorrow, same Bat-time, same --

Concrete umbrella: KLONK.

Penguin traps them in the amusement park shooting gallery with real guns instead of toys. That's because Penguin has class, ladies and gentlemen.

After they make their escape, Batman and Robin don't wait to beat up the Penguin and his henchfolk, they decide to regroup at the Batcave. These guys have legitimately committed actual crimes. Robin himself points out that he would have preferred to stay and pummel the bad guys.

Then Batman says, "On what charge?"

"On what charge?" This is a question that Batman asked. *Batman.*

Penguin insists that the police take the Dynamic Duo down, because they fought in public a couple of times, I guess.

Then the episode gets good, and by good, I mean hilarious.

I mean, more funny than the average already-pretty-funny Bat-episode.

Batman has a plan to nab Penguin. It involves Gotham police killing him and Robin in public after convincing Penguin that they have gone into a murderous rage.

Batman: Your super-brain power has driven us mad, Penguin!

Robin: Something snapped!

Batman: We don't care if we go up the river for a hundred years, we're getting you first!

Then the Gotham police gun down Batman and Robin in an alley, and Chief O'Hara and his men cover their bullet-riddled bodies with sheets.

We're still in Season One of this show, folks. There are literally dozens and dozens more episodes of this series.

As part of Batman's plan, he pulls a Bat-hole move of the worst proportion: He doesn't tell Alfred that he and Robin are alive. Alfred, who dusts his cave, feeds his ward and his aunt, and made up a top-notch pun when Commissioner Gordon called in the previous episode, believes Batman and Robin are dead. Then all he does is wipe a single tear from his eye. Alfred has grit.

Penguin steals the Batmobile and converts it to the Birdmobile, and millionaire heiress Sophia Starr agrees to marry him. At the wedding party, a sign clearly calls the wedding gifts "loot," which should have been a clue for Gotham sophisticates. At this point, I'm guessing Penguin's plan was to legitimately be given wedding gifts?

Penguin's mastery of crime is far beyond my understanding. Rest assured that it does involve umbrellas. Not concrete ones, but at least he's staying true to his creative muse.

Naturally, Penguin's plot doesn't work out, but it's not because it was a bad plan. Penguin just got overconfident, flush with success at his public acceptance and the public execution of his foes.

But all is not for naught, because Sophia Starr wants to keep going steady with Penguin, but he's not down with couplehood. That penguin has to waddle, and waddle free, except when the Gotham police trundle him off to prison.

Batman then says he will have to fumigate the Batmobile, which I would find insulting were I a tuxedo-wearing criminal who prided himself on his appearance.

Burgess Meredith's portrayal in this series has not been outdone. Pretty much all Bat-villains have been made over, rebooted, transformed, or refurbished since the *Batman* TV series, but it seems that every creator agrees that Penguin doesn't need fixing.

Every Penguin since then traces a direct line to Meredith's portrayal. Danny DeVito in *Batman Returns* added the fish-consuming grossness that would have scandalized 1960s TV. He also used penguins in his crimes, which seems like something Meredith's Penguin would have thought of. He used a giant clam in the second season. How did he overlook penguins?

Penguin: I need to use a creature in my clever crimes. But what? It seems as plain as the nose on my face, *wawk, wawk.*

Robin Lord Taylor's Penguin in *Gotham* took away the grossness and replaced it with sheer sadism and lunacy.

Meredith's persona gave pizzazz to the Penguin that has stuck with him. Style does not go out of style.

Unlike most of Batman's enemies, Penguin is not crazy. He's just weird, and if weirdness is a crime, then we should all go to jail. Also, if we put bombs and concrete in umbrellas and try to kill and rob people.

Joe Crowe is an Addy Award-winning freelance writer, copy editor, and proofreader (and he works cheap! Write him at joebcrowe at gmail dot com.) Joe is the co-director with Gary Mitchel of Dragon Con's American Sci-Fi Classics track, where they venture into the archives of sci-fi movie and TV history. He's also a pro wrestling announcer at Victory Championship Wrestling.

Joe is also the co-founder with Shane Ivey of RevolutionSF.com. He is one of the writers of White Rocket Books' *Assembled! Five Decades of Earth's Mightiest*, a book about the history of Marvel's Avengers in comics, TV, and movies.

Stefanie and Quin Crowe manage Joe's care and feeding in Fultondale, Alabama. His writing has been called "Swiftean in its satirical eloquence" and "the worst piece of garbage I have ever seen."

ZOWIE!

Spongepouch Batbelts

"The Ring of Wax/Give 'Em the Axe"
By Chris Franklin

Riddle me this: Who lives in a pineapple under the sea?

Answer: Spongepouch Batbelts

Now, before you skip this review for the next, hear me out. I evoked that earworm of a theme song only to make a point.

When most of the folks reading this book first encountered the *Batman* TV series, it was viewed upon fuzzy screens with often bad reception. Even if you had a then resplendent color television with the best picture of its day, it still pales to the ultra-HD/Blu-Ray/4K resolution we currently have access to. Also, the TV station broadcasting it might have not had the best print of any given episode. Multigenerational copies were passed from station to station around the world, and the visual and audio quality often suffered accordingly.

We made due, however. If we had to adjust those rabbit ears

or even smack the cabinet to get the optimal picture, it was still worth it to see our favorite heroes and their daring do. The sheer tingling excitement of that animated opening was enough to hook us every time.

Today, however, with the advancements in entertainment technology, we can see much more. Aspects of this beloved and obsessed-over series that were once hidden among the static lines and washed out transfer are now so obvious; a cursory view of our Blu-Ray sets is almost like shining a Bat-Signal upon them.

Take for instance Episode 23/24, "The Ring of Wax" and "Give 'Em the Axe", a return engagement with Frank Gorshin's Riddler that originally aired on March 30 and 31, 1966. The story by Jack Paritz and Bob Rodgers begins at the famous Madame Soleil Wax Museum (a nod to Madame Tussaud's) with the unveiling of a waxen figure of Gotham's most famous crimefighter. But when the curtain is drawn, instead of the Caped Crusader we find the wiry and waxy figure of the Prince of Puzzlers! Well, it's actually just Gorshin, standing VERY still (although he does sway a bit) with his face and hair slathered in shiny glycerin makeup to make him look slightly less than human, but still very creepy. A tape recorder at his feet taunts the patrons with two riddles, and then the Thompson submachine gun he's holding squirts out red paint on the upper-crust crowd. Director James B. Clark marks the first of his 15 Batman episodes with an artistic flourish as Gorshin actually shoots the camera (and the viewing audience) with his colored ammunition.

Informed of this, Commissioner Gordon tells Soleil that "we'll take care of it". Which of course means he phones for Batman and Robin. Bruce and Dick must abandon their game of South American capitals, much to the chagrin of Aunt Harriet, who gets a very small role in these episodes, but slightly bigger than Alfred. Clark frames the shot in Bruce's study differently than most, and we get a better look at the right hand wall, but unfortunately Dick's Batpole is completely obscured from this otherwise interesting angle. At Police HQ, the Dynamic Duo, Gordon and Chief O'Hara contemplate the meaning of the Riddler's latest conundrums; "What is black and white, and red all over", and "What has leaves, and no bark?" The ultimate answer leads them to the Gotham Public Library, but the greater question is...what's up with Batman's belt?

Something I'm sure *none* of us would have ever caught on our cabinet-encased family televisions is the strange variation of the classic Utility Belt that Batman is sporting here. Instead of the usual pouches that Adam West made fashionable, on either side of the polished metal bat-buckle rests... two yellow sponges. The bottom snaps that normally keep the usual faux leather-covered wooden props are there, but the pouches themselves? They are the same sponges your Mom was probably washing dishes with in the kitchen while you were glued to your TV set.

Why? Why switch out a custom-made prop with a household item? The truth is, I don't know. The reasons are lost to time, partially because few seemed to notice them in time to ask the cast and crew of the show when they were still with us. Perhaps it was so Adam West wouldn't take a block of wood to his ribs every time he bent over? I'm sure a belt full of lumber made for uncomfortable masked manhunting, but these replacements sure don't do much for practicality.

I will admit I didn't notice these myself firsthand, but after reading an article on MeTV's website posted in November of 2016 by Peter Greenwood, I can't *unsee* them, every time they show up. And this isn't the only episode we see them in either, although they are in practically every scene!

The action shifts to the Riddler's hideout at the Kandle Lite Candle Factory, and we are introduced to Gorshin's Goon Squad, Tallow (played by a pre-*Beverly Hills, 90210* Joey Tata), Matches (prolific character actor Michael Greene), and Moth, the Moll de jour. One look at Linda Scott's costume and you can't help but look past the actress (later known for a memorable guest spot on the final episodes of *The Green Hornet* and the original film version of *Westworld*) and ahead to *Batman* Season Three. Yes, it seems Scott is sporting the prototype for Yvonne Craig's iconic purple besparkled Batgirl uniform. Blink and you may miss the Batman costume seen on the manikin Tallow and Matches are disassembling and melting down. This episode, like many of the first season, is shrouded in shadows, creating a very noirish atmosphere the show will soon lose. Turns out the Batmanikin is made of a "Revolutionary New Ring of Wax Universal Solvent," illegal contraband courtesy of bees from the Cognac district of France, with the ability to burn through steel vaults!

At the library, The King of Conundrums continues his waxen war using the ring of wax solvent to burn through the conveniently labeled "Vault of Rare Old Books". Look closely and you'll see the orange color of the wax rub off on Gorshin's hands. Downstairs at the circulation desk, Batman and Robin encounter librarian Miss Prentice, who is so excited to see the Dynamic Duo, she breaks her occupational vow of silence, and Batman has to remind her to keep the volume down. Actress Elizabeth Harrower will fill the same position in Season Three's premiere, "Enter Batgirl, Exit Penguin" playing Drusilla, a colleague of head librarian Barbara Gordon. But who's to say they aren't the same character, one named Drusilla Prentice?

Upstairs, the Riddler has already found his objective. *The Lost Treasure of the Incas* will supposedly lead the criminal mastermind to the fabled loot, resulting in one of Gorshin's most memorable outbursts, a series of "HUZZAHs". Batman and Robin enter the vault and are surprisingly held at gunpoint by Matches and aerosol can-point by the Riddler. Batman knocks the gun out of the goon's hand, but it does manage to fire, a rare instance of gunplay on the series. A mini-Bat-fight breaks out, and it's now very obvious when slightly out-of-shape stuntman Hubie Kearns and clearly middle-aged stunt coordinator Victor Paul substitute for Batman and Robin, respectively.

West and Ward are back in the shot when Gorshin sprays their boots with "Dr. Riddler's Instant Forever Stick Invisible Wax Emulsion". The Caped Crusaders are stuck to the floor, and not even the now VERY OBVIOUS absorbent sponges Batman is packing can soak up this mess. You can even make out some of their large porous holes as Batman uses his laser gun to melt the Riddler's sticky trap, who escapes behind a smoke screen leaving another riddle: "The more you take away, the larger it grows. He also leaves behind the answer, a hole, right in the vault wall. Batman finds a waxy residue on the edges of the hole, and races back to the Batcave to analyze it.

In their subterranean HQ, the Duo determine Riddler left the wax residue as a clue, and that its chemical composition of Sodium, Uranium (!) and Nitrogen, point toward the word "sun". And the French word for sun is "soleil" as in Madame Soleil and her Wax Museum, where this candle was first lit. Their logic, while perhaps a bit hard to swallow, is nonetheless solid, as are Batman's belt pouches, now back to the usual wood and leather-like composition, as the two race off to the museum.

At the eerily atmospheric "House of Wax", our heroes pass glycerin-coated actors playing figures of Jack the Ripper and a rather familiar-looking American Revolutionary War display before examining the Riddler's party-crashing dummy, played in long shots by Gorshin stunt double Eddie Hice. Gorshin himself makes his presence known when in the guise of a revolutionary fifer he turns his wind instrument into a blowgun that shoots drugged darts in the back of our heroes, who don't hear the omniscient warnings of narrator Desmond Doomsday.

After taking time to admire his wax figure (to the strains of some romantic musical cues!), Riddler and his gang load the Defeated Duo into their Kandle Lite van. It's then that Riddler eyes another prize he hadn't considered: the Batmobile. Having been defeated by the crafty car's anti-theft devices in the pilot, a pair of needle-nose pliers is all it takes to disarm the advanced security system this time. When the cunning auto thief presses the ignition button, we can see how hastily crafted it is. It almost appears to have been carved out of wood with a pocketknife, and never sanded. Somewhat disappointing to see on the greatest car in film or television history.

When the stolen Batmobile and van arrive at the candle factory, Riddler remarks "We better get our everyday clothes back on; we look too suspicious this way". Because green question marked tights are subtle. Oh, and if you missed the Bat-sponges before, they are at their most apparent as the Knocked-out Knight awakens in the van. They honestly look a bit dirty! Moth doesn't notice the cleaning utensils, but instead is smitten with Batman's Pure West physique. Riddler scolds her that the arch-criminal business is no place for such emotions. It's nearly the end of this episode, so of course our heroes find themselves in a death trap. Although this one is a little more straightforward than many of the more…inventive ones we'll see later in the series. The Dynamic Duo is suspended by their wrists over a large vat conveniently labeled "ENORMOUS CANDLE DIPPER". The wax angle is new, but the vat is not. In fact, nearly 10 years earlier, *The Adventures of Superman* paid homage to this old serial gag in one of its last episodes with George Reeves hanging over a vat of acid.

His World's Finest pal is now feeling the heat however, because Batman is sweating! Certainly something unnoticeable before the digital age was (gasp!) Batman's armpit stains! Yes, the idol of millions is caught in need of some Bat-antiperspirant, with dark blotches clearly visible in the underarm area of his tights. In Bob Garcia's and Joe Desris' *Batman: A Celebration of the Classic TV Series*, West reminisced about how series Costume Designer and Wardrobe Manager Jan Kemp was the show's greatest stain fighter. "Try to do action scenes under hot lights and not show sweat through the tunic. Jan had to use a hairdryer on my chest between takes. It looked a little silly but it quickly became ordinary." Apparently, even Kemp could make mistakes, because Batman is breaking the "never let them see you sweat" motto here.

Also visible to the now more discerning eye are the wires which are actually holding West and Ward in place, no doubt for comfort and safety, since they are actually suspended quite high above the studio floor. Riddler taunts his prey, then orders Matches to begin lowering the Caped Crimefighters into the vat, slowly, so he can savor every inch of their descent, on their way to becoming immortalized in wax…the hard way.

As they drop, the Dynamic Duo riddles the Riddler with questions about his crime spree thus far. With the usual insane intensity in his blue-gray eyes, he tells them the book contains an ancient riddle that will lead him right to the fabled lost treasure of the Incas. Batman scoffs at the treasure's existence as only a legend, but Riddler is convinced it's real, and also convinced the heroes won't be around to see it!

Part Two, "Give 'Em the Axe", begins as the Riddler continues to watch his enemies' impending demise in rapt attention, gloating that the lost Incan treasure is worth millions. Even as he nears death, the Caped Crusader offers wisdom to the man who is slowly killing him; "Remember Riddler, you can't buy friends with money". Unmoved by this advice, the Puzzling Prince rapidly retorts "With money who needs friends?"

Interestingly, up to this point, the villains are actually staying to witness the Dynamic Duo's death in person, not following the Rogues Gallery union laws which state all death traps must be left to follow through with their eventual and inevitable conclusion, unsupervised. Luckily, the fumes from the wax begin to irritate Moth and then the rest of the crew, so the Riddler begrudgingly orders them to leave the room to witness his triumph from his candle-scope below.

With the villains away, the minds of Batman and Robin are at play, thinking of a way to escape their impending demise. The keen and educated mind of the World's Greatest Detective notes a large metal barrel of liquid, very clearly labeled with its chemical composition. He deduces it is the solution for treating candlewicks, which is highly explosive when exposed to heat. In their low-lit basement hideaway, Riddler and his gang pull down the candle-scope, which of course looks like a large candle in its holder, complete with wax running down the periscope shaft, and ringed handles. One wonders, why the Kandle Lite factory would have such a contraption.

It is then that Batman notices a shaft of sunlight penetrating through a hole in the factory roof. He reflects that light off of his highly polished belt buckle onto the liquid, hoping to ignite the combustible chemicals. As he turns his body, the light blinds Riddler watching from below. Batman moves into the optimum position, and an animated yellow spotlight floats across the barrel to the pool of liquid inside. A large explosion erupts, although it looks to be directly beneath our heroes, not from the side of the vat as it should be.

Riddler and goons feel the shock, and as the Prince of Puzzlers observes the aftermath with the candle-scope, he finds the seemingly lifeless bodies of the Caped Crusaders strewn on the factory floor. Gorshin pushes his faces so far into the rubber bezel of the periscope I'm surprised it didn't leave a mark, as he delivers one of his best moments of evil glee, gloating over the demise of the Despised Duo. Moth is far more practical and wants to get back to that whole Incan treasure plot, but first Riddler must call Commissioner Gordon, and tell him his good news, with a riddle of course. When Moth questions this course of action, her disgusted boss reminds her "Crime is no fun without riddles. I'll have you know that's the main reason I took up this crime game." It's a rare moment of insight into the origins of the villains on the series, and shines a spotlight on Riddler's particular form of mania.

Riddler informs the top cop that his champions are dead, and a shaken Neil Hamilton delivers his vengeful ultimatum with gusto; "If you had anything to do with this Riddler, I'll track you down to the ends of the earth, and that's a solemn promise!" Of course, both we and the Riddler know the well-meaning Gordon couldn't catch a cold, so the arch-fiend rolls his eyes before riddling once more; "What has four legs, runs day and night, but never gets anywhere". However, our Duo is still Dynamic, not Deceased, and they come to on the factory floor, then race outside to the Batmobile which the Riddler has left behind. Batman phones Gordon, who is relieved that his trusted ally is still among the living. He tells them of the new riddle, and they ruminate its meaning in the cockpit. In full view is the handle of the clearly-labeled "Emergency Bat-Turn Lever", which here seems to be made of a dark red rubber material with sparkly fleck. As always the two work out the riddle through back-and-forth banter, and deduce the answer is the Gotham City

Museum, even though, as Robin points out, its lion fountains aren't currently running right now, due to a water shortage.

When we see the exterior of the museum, the lions are indeed waterless, although they don't really look much like fountains anyhow. In the museum's storage basement, Riddler and his themed thugs search for a sarcophagus amidst a room full of medieval torture devices. Moth is spooked by them, but a somewhat turned-on Riddler describes the maiden's bath, the hanging iron mask, the wheel of death, the rack and the stocks (although this device is actually called a pillory). Outside, Batman and Robin (or Batman and Victor Paul, since it's definitely not Ward) arrive at the museum in the Batmobile, which has a new accessory hanging on its undercarriage, but more on that later. When the scene cuts to close-ups of West and Ward, Batman has seriously upgraded his spongy-belt. A sign announces "On Display, Starting Monday, Sarcophagus of Haulpo Cuisi, Ancient Incan Emperor". Robin notes Aunt Harriet was reading an article about the exhibit earlier that morning. The museum was building an airtight case to display the sarcophagus, lest the mummy be exposed to air, and crumble to dust. Batman deduces that the Incan treasure is hidden in the sarcophagus, and the Riddler knows it.

They find the obviously flimsy doors of the museum locked, and Batman forgets he's carrying a laser gun. Maybe he left it in the sponge belt? Robin notices a small window open and begs Batman to let him go through it. Batman notes "It's dangerous", like actively pursuing deranged and often-armed criminals isn't. He agrees to let a Boy Wonder do a Batman's job, and pulls a Batarang from the large wedge-shape holster on this belt, and attaches it to a Bat-rope pulled from the even larger box reel riding his hip. No wonder he prefers the sponges! Robin climbs the wall, keeping in touch on his "throat communicator" while Batman talks to him on his more traditional twin-antenna hand-held device. Burt Ward is really selling that climbing this wall is no easy task, in great contrast to how the two will later glide through their fabled celebrity-filled Bat-Climbs. Always civic-minded, Batman worries about what the Riddler's potentially disastrous actions may do to foreign relations with our neighbors to the south.

Now inside, Robin is nabbed by Tallow and Matches after a brief tussle. Outside, Batman should be more comfortable since he's traded in bulky belt apparatus for sponges once more, but he's worried about his ward, who is now incommunicado. Robin is brought before Riddler, who is shocked to see him among the living. The sly Boy Wonder smartly informs the Prince of Puzzlers that Batman is indeed dead, and threatens revenge. Riddler responds by ordering him tied to the rack. Moth, once again is concerned for her enemy's safety.

Batman is also concerned, and pulls the Batmobile around back to the loading dock doors. He calls Gordon for backup, then pulls the very roughly-hewn Bat-ram lever. The red half-circle shape is obviously made of unsanded wood with a simple screw attaching the handle, and a coat of red paint hastily slapped on. The silver and bronze studded Bat-ram pops from under the front bumper. Clark does another neat straight-toward-the-camera shot as the ram fills the screen, and the Batmobile bursts through the museum doors.

Tallow gives Robin a bit of a stretch on the rack, and Riddler's joy is multiplied when Matches finds their quarry, which of course is marked "Ancient Incan Sarcophagus, DO NOT EXPOSE CONTENTS TO AIR". Bringing things full circle, Riddler pulls out the Ring of Wax Universal Solvent, and places it on the metal trunk containing the casket. As he places the lit candle next to it, he laments that Batman is unable to see his moment of victory. The intricate hemming on Gorshin's mask is evident here, proving it's no mere Halloween accessory, but a fully realized piece of costuming. The gloating goons look up to see the shadow of a bat cast over them and shriek, turning to face the shrouded form of Batman, holding his cape like wings! A moody moment straight from the Golden Age of comics, fully and sincerely realized.

Batman swings on a lamp into the goons (a stunt that never gets old) as our final Bat-fight begins. Note the lack of extra lackeys appearing out of nowhere, a hallmark of later episodes. While Robin watches the fight helplessly, the Ring of Wax solvent gets hotter and hotter, burning slowly through the sarcophagus' trunk. Batman puts Tallow in the pillory, Matches in the iron mask, and Moth in the maiden's bath before finally extinguishing the candle. Riddler attacks with a sword, but after only a few dodges, Batman beats the blade out of his opponent's grip. The Caped Crusader then gets a bit more brutal than usual, grabbing Riddler's hand and twisting his arm, while squeezing his fingers with a rather sickening, crunching sound. Riddler cowers and begs as Batman demands he give up his evil ways, and leads him to the wheel of death. The Darker-than-usual Knight even growls at the simpering super villain, tying him to the wheel, and giving him a spin (or his stunt double, anyway).

Batman frees Robin, and when telling his young ward a nourishing meal will help him feel better, he rather carelessly namedrops Aunt Harriet! It's then that Chief O'Hara and the boys in blue arrive. The Riddler they begin to untie is obviously NOT Frank Gorshin, even by fuzzy old TV broadcast standards! O'Hara tells Batman that they accidentally went to the wax museum first (begorah!), and then Batman, still wearing his sponges, helps Moth from her bath. There's irony in there somewhere.

Moth confesses to the hero she's learned her lesson; crime doesn't pay. A stern but disappointed Batman responds; "Unfortunately you learned your lesson too late Moth. A Moth that plays around candles is bound to be burned." As he is taken away, Riddler declares their war isn't over.

But it is all over but the coda, anyway, which finds Bruce, Dick and Aunt Harriet taking in the mummy exhibit. Aunt Harriet marvels at his preservation, while Bruce whispers to Dick: "The old boy nearly didn't make it."

One wonders why Jack Paritz and Bob Rodgers didn't contribute any further scripts to the series. They seem to have a handle on the precarious balance of humor and action, unless we can chalk that up to Lorenzo Semple, Jr.'s possible script doctoring. Regardless, the end result is a strong outing for the show, and another great showcase for Gorshin's wonderfully manic Riddler. The regular cast is still fully committed to the farce of playing everything deadly serious and straight. Which can't be easy to do...when you're wearing sponges on your hips.

Despite such strange idiosyncrasies being very noticeable now, what is even more evident is the craft that went into every aspect of the show, creating a larger than life world that kids wanted to live in, and adults wanted to laugh at. But ultimately, it's the delivery and performance of the actors, in particular West and Ward, that allows episodes like this to shine today, no matter the level of scrutiny. Their talent and charisma are obvious, no matter if your TV picture is fuzzy UHF, or crystal clear HD.

Chris Franklin is a writer, illustrator, graphic designer and podcaster who has contributed to *Back Issue* and *Retro Fan* magazines, as well as 13th Dimension.com. He co-hosts various podcasts on the Fire and Water Podcast Network, including *Batman: Knightcast* with Ryan Daly, *Superman Movie Minute* with Rob Kelly, and with his wife Cindy co-hosts and produces *Super Mates* and *JLUCast.* He proudly hangs a print of the 1966 *Batman* movie poster on his living room wall, signed by Adam West and Frank Gorshin.

ZOK!

When Is a Joke Not a Joke? When It's a Riddle of a Story

"The Joker Trumps an Ace/Batman Sets the Pace"

By Alan J. Porter

"A joke: What are fur mink skins used for more than anything else?"
"To hold minks together."

This truly awful joke, uttered by the Joker in the pre-credit sequence of "The Joker Trumps an Ace," is symptomatic of why I find this particular storyline so troubling. For a start, it's not a joke—it's clearly a riddle—and it's delivered to a captured selection of Gotham's wealthiest shoppers, who are huddled together in a furriers shop under the watchful eye of The Joker and his goons.

I'm not the only one who thinks that this poor attempt at a joke, which is an equally poor riddle, is indicative of some behind-the-scenes confusion. During their review of this storyline, the hosts of the Batcave podcast[1] speculated that this may have originally been a Riddler story that had been adapted into a Joker escapade.

Personally, I think it's emblematic of a deeper issue involving the Joker himself. Who is this Joker? Is he a thief, a con-man, an anarchist, a killer, a kidnapper? Or is he just a random crazy dude? I don't believe that the producers felt they had a true handle on who the Crown Prince of Crime was at this early point in the series. While it's clear, from the opening animated credits, that he was meant to be a focal point of the show (he's the only villain to appear twice in the sequence), he was overshadowed by the Riddler (who surprisingly doesn't appear in the credits) once the series was under way.

Frank Gorshin's Riddler opened the 1966 *Batman* show with a story that cemented his character as a manic menace, but one with well-thought-out schemes and objectives. The early foundation of the character is undoubtedly helped by the fact that, up until the opening episode, The Riddler had only had three appearances in *Batman* comics; he wasn't an established presence in the Caped Crusader's mythos, so whatever was presented on the TV show was quickly established as the definitive interpretation of the character. Our friend The Joker, meanwhile, had been a pretty constant presence in the comics for most of the previous twenty-six years of publication. There had been multiple versions and interpretations of who the character was, so there was no definitive Joker, and that is reflected in the way the TV show struggled to get a grasp of what its Joker would be. It could be argued that his inconsistency is part of the Joker's character, and even Robin notes, later in this story, that the key to understanding The Joker is that "He never means what he seems to mean." If that had been acknowledged and played with as a character trait from early on, it may have helped.

The Joker, as presented here, is still poorly defined. In fact, he comes across as almost Riddler-lite (although I've heard it argued the other way—that The Riddler is Joker-lite).

Let's examine this two-part story in more detail.

The shopping expedition of several wealthy Gothamites is inter-

[1] *http://thebatcavepodcast.libsyn.com/episode-13-the-joker-trumps-an-acebatman-sets-the-pace*

rupted by the appearance of their "friendly neighborhood[2] hold-up man" and his gang. At first, it looks like The Joker has murder on his mind, as the shoppers are gathered together in the center of the store and his goons all point machine guns at them. But as the victims quake in terror, the guns are fired, releasing streamers of ribbon that bind them. So perhaps the objective is robbery? Yes, but it doesn't involve furs, or even the expensive jewelry on display around the necks of the female patrons. Instead, The Joker singles out the wife of Mr. Prescott-Belmont, of the banking Belmonts, and uses a giant magnet to steal a single hairpin from her head.

We soon learn from Commissioner Gordon that this is the second baffling robbery committed by The Joker in recent days, as it's also been reported that he has stolen a hole from a golf course. These are oddly meaningless crimes with no apparent connection between them; that again seems more like a riddle to me.

We cut to Wayne Manor, where Bruce Wayne and Dick Grayson are working on a jigsaw puzzle which has been turned upside down to hide the picture, as a way to train Dick's visual memory. Often, these Wayne Manor set-ups have some implied connection or synchronicity with the crime about to be committed. So why a puzzle? Doesn't this again suggest a Riddler plot rather than a Joker-driven one? Unusually, the set-up never pays off, as the new skill is not used at any point in the story.

The Dynamic Duo arrives at Gordon's office shortly after a mysterious large parcel is delivered, wrapped in brown paper. Batman examines the parcel with a stethoscope, presumably retrieved from his utility belt, before slashing the string holding it together with a folding knife that is clearly too large for the belt pocket in which it's located.

It's at this point that we get an appearance of the folding Bat-Shield—which is, for some reason, conveniently sitting just below the edge of the table where the parcel is located. While it's meant to be suggested that Batman somehow produces this large piece of equipment from his utility belt, Adam West's lean and reach maneuver to pick it up from under the table is plainly obvious. The

[2] *An interesting turn of phrase that catches the ear today, even though this episode aired eighteen months before the debut of the iconic 1967* Spider-Man *cartoon show.*

converse is just as obvious when Burt Ward folds the shield up and makes a gesture as though to slip it under Robin's cape but clearly just drops it to the floor behind the table.

The parcel contains an inflatable genie-type figure that again appears to have no connection to the other crimes. In the box is a small recording machine carrying a message from The Joker that seems to indicate that he knows exactly when Gordon summoned Batman, as he assumes Batman is "there by now." This goes unremarked as we then transition to the core of the message: "Did you hear what the maid said when the duchess asked if she'd given the goldfish fresh water that morning? 'No your highness[3], he hasn't yet used what he had yesterday.'" Robin points out the key to the Joker's twisted mind is that the joke doesn't mean what it seems to mean. I will submit that this one is less of a riddle and more of a joke, but like Commissioner Gordon points out, it's not a very funny one. In fact, it's an incredibly contrived and meaningless one designed to suggest two things, royalty and gold. At this point, even the law-enforcement characters begin to agree with me that this incarnation of The Joker isn't acting normal, for in response to the joke clue, Gordon points out that "It's not like The Joker to help us catch him."

Batman makes one of his incredible script-driven leaps of logic that connects the hole stolen from the golf course and the stupid joke to a newspaper story about the visiting Maharajah of Nimpah. According to the article, the Maharajah is so rich he plays golf with jewel-encrusted solid-gold clubs, and he's scheduled to play in one hour at the same country club from which The Joker stole the hole.

Instead of a simple scene transition, we actually get some short footage of the Batmobile on the streets of downtown Gotham as Batman and Robin make their way to the "exclusive Winitoto Country Club." There, "a sinister figure looms above the fairway" as The Joker is seen checking out the course; we assume he is checking on the whereabouts of the aforementioned Maharajah. Satisfied, The Joker and his gang make a hasty retreat to a conspicuously parked blue van adorned with the slogan, "Let GAYFELLOW take you to the CLEANERS." The apparent reference to a company called

[3] *An etiquette* faux pas *by the writers, as a duchess would not be addressed by a servant as "your highness." The correct form of address is "your grace" or "madam."*

Gayfellow Cleaners is a complete non sequitur, as neither of the two business premises the gang will later use as hideouts are cleaners. So why the name? Is the "gayfellow" a riff on the Joker, or is it, as some have suggested, a nod to Cesar Romero's Hollywood status as a "confirmed bachelor"? Maybe the "take you to the cleaners" tag line is also a nod to the slang for committing a robbery. Or maybe I'm just reading way too much into things.

Batman's arrival at the club is accompanied by an observation from one club member that "Crime is certainly rampant these days," an indication that to the citizens of Gotham City, the arrival of the Caped Crusaders is always an indication of foul play in progress. The club president, who happens to be Prescott-Belmont, greets Batman with the immortal line, "Batman, I presume." Presume? Who else would be in Batman's costume? With the Dynamic Duo inconspicuously looking on from behind an umbrella pole via the smallest pair of Bat-binoculars, we meet the target of all this chicanery: the Maharajah of Nimpah.

Even by the standards of the mid1960s, this is one of the most inappropriate and culturally insensitive mocking portrayals that rolls out all the stereotypes it possibly can around a large, rich, Indian potentate. As the game on the first hole reaches a climax, a cloud of gas is triggered from the hole, incapacitating the players. At first, it seems that The Joker's men are just after the clubs, but then we see the royal visitor being hauled up and transferred into the back of the cleaners' van. What was an apparent robbery is now a kidnapping. To the Batmobile!

With the Batmobile giving chase across the course fairways, the van suddenly disappears, and the Batmobile comes to a halt, stopping just short of running over a miniature model of the phantom van. Within the van awaits another bad joke as a clue: "Did you hear about the kid who wanted to sell his dog for $50,000? He traded it for two $25,000 cats but you can't make a deal like that for the Maharajah because we've got plenty of cats already." This somehow enables Batman to make an incredible piece of deductive reasoning that The Joker is hiding out in an old refinery once owned by "Katz, Katz, Katz & Company."

Inside, The Joker and his gang are setting up a staged card game, where we are introduced to his moll Jill, who appears to be preening in one of the stolen furs from the store where they didn't rob anything! Batman's and Robin's Batarangs bounce off a mirror on the side the van and, realizing that the Joker has turned the tables on them, they are now trapped. As the gang ties them up, Joker starts to sing a strange little number:

"Now swing that twine / and warp these guests of mine /
No more will they scoff / we'll cut their circulation off /
If they do not see the joke / pull the ropes and let them choke!"

Since when did the Joker sing? It's another strangely off-character moment that makes no sense in terms of either the story or the development of the villain himself.

It seems that the Joker is set to take the opportunity to rid himself of his nemesis once and for all, but following pleas from Jill, who has taken a liking to Batman's physique, he suddenly decides to give them a sporting chance, much to the annoyance of one of his goons. After using his convenient plot device, a "funny ray that neutralizes the gadgets in the utility belts for at least an hour," The Joker ushers our heroes into a furnace smoke stack and asks them if they could remain afloat for an hour. If they can, he promises to let them go free.

But what's this? It's a trick! The stack doesn't start to fill up with water, but rather a deadly gas. The narrator asks, "Is this The Joker's crowning jest?", and we fade out and wait to see what fate awaits the Caped Crusader and his chum.

In Part 2, no gadgets are required as Batman and Robin link arms back to back and walk their way up the chimney stack. They pause only to give the Joker an ironic wave as they pass by, just as he is in full monologue mode, acknowledging their courage and how life will be much simpler with them out of the way. The Joker concludes his soliloquy with instructions to his goons to pump the gas out of the chimney, adding, "Some passerby might get killed." Well, that's a change from the Joker we know today. Far from being a homicidal maniac, he is focused on stealing stuff and little more (with the sole exception of trying to rid himself of Batman and Robin, apparently).

Back at the Batcave, our heroes examine the golf course hole and hair-pin, presumably having stopped by the country club once more to retrieve them. The convenient gas analyzer and accompanying manual link the type of gas used to just a single source in Gotham: the Ferguson Novelty and Magician Supply Company. So what sort of novelty shop stocks knockout gas? It's at this point that the "world's greatest detective" begins to suspect that all may not be what it seems regarding the kidnap victim.

Bruce and Dick leave the costumes at home and visit the novelty shop, where an assistant delivers some of the best technobabble this side of the USS *Enterprise*, as she explains how a prism can be used to counteract the effects of a one-way mirror. She then casually leaves the prism aside, enabling Bruce to use it to peer through the mirror into The Joker's hidden lair behind the store, where we see the relaxed Maharajah. So is the girl in the joke shop part of The Joker's crew? Is this a set-up to lure Batman into trying another rescue? It sure seems like it—but if so, how did she know to give the prism to Bruce Wayne, unless The Joker knows that Batman and Bruce are one and the same? I've had a long-held theory that this is the case, but that The Joker doesn't really care; as far as he is concerned, in and out of the costume his nemesis is just Batman. To him, Bruce Wayne is irrelevant[4].

The joke shop scene stands out for another, probably totally coincidental, reason. Dick Grayson is seen playing with a pair of wind-up teeth, and he asks Bruce, "Who does this remind you of?" It's clearly a reference to their current foe, The Joker. But it does make me wonder whether that was picked up from this scene and used to inform, or possibly inspire, The Joker's post-mortem practical gag with the joke teeth at the conclusion of Tim Burton's 1989 *Batman* movie.

We return to the Batcave, where—with the help of a hand-drawn "photograph" of the joke shop, some more incredible leaps of logic, and the worst example of applied trigonometry in TV history—Bat-

[4] *But that's probably the subject for another essay*

man concludes that there is a ventilation shaft that leads to the store room he'd spotted through the one-way mirror. This can only mean one thing: it's time for the Dynamic Duo to drop in on The Joker and his goons.

The Joker strangely greets our heroes, demanding, "What's the matter with you, Batman, I'm the funny man around here." Perhaps this is in reaction to a line that was later cut. He seems low-key and unwilling to get involved in the classic exchange of "Pows" and "Biffs" that follow, before he and Jill escape to leave the rest of the gang to be rounded up. But where is the Maharajah?

It seems that the potentate has developed a liking for the "bandit-Joker" and willingly, via a radio message to police headquarters, asks that Batman be on hand at Gotham Bank to help him cash a personal check for $500,000 to pay his own ransom.

The main players convene at the Gotham Bank, where we find that the president is none other than Prescott-Belmont. The Maharajah asks Batman to personally endorse the check, and just in case the audience doesn't get the significance of this, O'Hara helpfully comments on "it being a sad day for Batman being forced to use his name for a criminal payoff." Gordon adds, to further emphasize the point, "This will tarnish his image considerably."

But wait! What's this? Batman poking the royal visitor with a Bat-dart? Why doesn't the Maharajah respond? What trickery is this? All is revealed when Batman jams the Bat-dart in harder and is rewarded with a familiar squeal. A fight ensues, during which the Maharajah's body suit and mask are ripped off to reveal the presence of none other than The Joker himself. As Robin reminds O'Hara, the key to The Joker's twisted mind is that "He never means what he seems to mean." And I'll be honest, I have no idea how this line, foreshadowed in the opening episode, plays out in this story at all.

As Batman points out, no one had seen The Joker and the Maharajah in the same place at the same time. Nice job giving the police a clue as to how to solve the mystery of the man beneath the cowl there, Batman! He also points out that there had been no official protest at the supposed disappearance of the royal visitor from the Nimpah embassy.

The coda to this story is one of the strangest in the whole series, and not just for Aunt Harriet's offensive and out-of-character joke at the expense of the real Maharajah of Nimpah. Alfred is startled, and apparently annoyed, that the Bat-phone rings again so quickly after his charges have just returned from a case. It seems there is an expectation that crime in this Gotham runs to a schedule, allowing its protectors some down-time between adventures. But there is no crime in progress—it's Commissioner Gordon, asking Batman about a rumor that he is leaving Gotham to go to California to run for Governor. Batman assures Gordon that "As long as there's a criminal at large in Gotham City, wild horses couldn't drag me away." It's a fitting sentiment to conclude on, but a strange non sequitur of a question[5].

When you look back on this two-parter, the story is about an elaborate con-game that The Joker is playing to get hold of half a million dollars in cash, while at the same time disgracing Batman and repeatedly humiliating Prescott-Belmont. To pull off the con, as played out on screen, would have taken a lot of planning, including setting up a golf game with the major and planting a newspaper story in the right edition for Batman to read. If part of his original plan was to disgrace Batman, then why does he try to kill him in the smoke stack? Or did that part come later, following Batman's escape? As for the periodic and less than coincidental appearance of the banker/country club president, what was the Joker's beef with him, anyway? It's never alluded to. Overall, the two episodes that make up this story are something of a riddle.

So when is The Joker not The Joker? For most of this story, it turns out. Even though it's his third outing in the role, and although we see some flashes of the Crown Prince of Crime we will come to know, both the showrunners and Cesar Romero are still struggling to separate The Joker from The Riddler at this point and define who, or what, he is. Here, he runs the gamut of thief, con-man, sportsman, risk-taker, and more, all without settling on any one role. And maybe that's the point, but it seems ill-thought-out and weakly executed in comparison to his question-mark-adorned compatriot. This

[5] *The battle for the governorship of California was hot news in 1966, but this topical, Hollywood-centric reference is completely out of place and certainly doesn't date well.*

is The Joker's last appearance in the first season, which may be an indication that the writers were still struggling with the character. For me, it's the between-seasons movie in which the relationships, differences, and characterizations of the two punsters of the *Batman '66* universe start to gel. It will be another fourteen stories and well in to season two before The Joker reappears, and from that point on, he becomes one of the most recurring villains, with another five stories spread throughout the rest of season two and in season three.

By the series' conclusion, Romero had made The Joker his own and laid the foundation for pretty much every live-action or animated version of the character from that point forward, with his manic whooping, cackling laugh, over-the-top behavior, quirky exaggerated mannerisms, and bold sweeping gestures. But at this early stage, he's little more than a bumbling buffoon.

Alan J. Porter's obsession with the Batman goes back to those heady days of 1966, and was rekindled in the early 1980s resulting in an insanely large Bat collection, the publication of *"The Unofficial BATMAN Collectors Guide,"* and eleven years of the *Gotham Gazette* website and the associated *Gotham Weekly News* newsletter service. The website and newsletter are no-more and the collection now dispersed, with a large proportion to be found at the Toy and Action Figure Museum in Pauls Valley, OK., but the on-line Bat presence continues with the *Batman On The Cover* blog on Tumblr (https://www.tumblr.com/blog/batmanonthecover) and Instagram (https://www.instagram.com/batmanonthecover). Outside of the Bat related stuff, he writes historical adventure fiction, pop-culture essays and books, as well as the occasional comic. More info can be found at http://alanjporter.com, or on twitter @alanjporter.

ZLONK!

Tut, Tut, the Pharaoh is a Nut

"The Curse of Tut/The Pharaoh's in a Rut"
By Robert Greenberger

The Riddler, the Penguin, the Joker, Mr. Freeze, the Mad Hatter, and False Face. They'd all matched wits with the Caped Crusader in comics and then on ABC's 1966 television series, but Batman had never before seen the likes of King Tut. That's because he was the series' first totally original criminal. One could argue that was Zelda the Great, who had shown up a few weeks earlier, but Zelda's story was derived from "Batman's Inescapable Doom-Trap!" (*Detective Comics* #346), with Zelda replacing a man named Carnado. No, my friends, King Tut was wholly original and perfectly fit the show's world of costumed criminals.

The product of writers Robert C. Dennis and Earl Barret, King Tut was made memorable thanks entirely to the performance of Victor Buono, who wasn't even the first actor considered for the part. Who that was remains lost to the ages, although *TV Guide* erroneously reported Robert Morse was up for the part, which could have been interesting, but nowhere near as much fun.

Let's turn back the calendar to February 1966, when the show was just a month old and the world was at the beginning of Batmania. ABC, Greenway Productions, and DC Comics had no clue they were going to strike a nerve. After all, *Batman* had been rushed into production the previous fall to fill a hole in the schedule, and ABC had marketed it as just one of several new shows in their freshly coined "Second Season." All producers William Dozier and Howie Horwitz knew were that they needed filmable scripts—and fast.

Dennis and Barret nicely fit the bill, given their individual and collaborative efforts throughout the years. Dennis had previously handled traditional prime-time drama (*The Untouchables* and *Perry Mason*), while also exploring the fantastical with *The Outer Limits*. He'd go on to write two episodes of the sci-fi-esque *Search*, as well as a pair of tales for *The Six Million Dollar Man*. His frequent partner mostly wrote sitcoms, such as ABC's *F Troop*, but would collaborate with Dennis on seven episodes of the imaginative *Wild Wild West*.

They landed the assignment and delivered a final-draft script dated February 28. Where did Tut come from—Dozier or the writers? There is no record of how this happened, although it was a stroke of genius, as the Egyptian motif fit Batman's world and was a nice complement to the other villains. So memorable was King Tut, in fact, that he was one of the few to appear in all three seasons, and was the only original mixed in with the fearsome foursome of Joker, Penguin, Riddler, and Catwoman.

Making his directorial debut was the veteran Charles R. Rondeau (1917–1996), who toggled between sitcoms including *F Troop* and soon thereafter would handle three episodes of William Daniels' heroic *Captain Nice*, six dramatic *Mission: Impossibles*, and even one *Wonder Woman*. When the producers and Rondeau settled on Buono, they had struck gold. Dozer was quoted in *Batman: A Celebration of the Classic TV Series* as saying, "Between [producer] Howie Horwitz and me, we just decided that Buono looked the part of big Arab king. He was marvelous, and so was that beard. Although the part was not created for him, we knew he was Tut as soon as we saw him."

In the same book, makeup designer Bruce Huchinson recalled,

"The first time we made him up, they wanted this exotic Egyptian-looking makeup on him. Well, we did the makeup. He looked like some old opera diva. [Buono] said laughing, 'I [can't] go out of this trailer looking like this.' So we just washed his face and put this little chin piece on and the costuming, and he sold it."

Shooting occurred in March, and by then, Batmania had the nation in its tight grip. As a result, associate producer William D'Angelo recalled that location shooting became a nightmare. The exterior sequences were shot in Ranchero Park, and he described thousands of people flocking to watch. Extra police were required to handle the masses, but they were easily outnumbered.

The episode is interesting in a number of respects. First, it plays with dual identities. You have Bruce Wayne and Batman being one man doing little to disguise the fact. In a meta moment early on, Commissioner Gordon first talks to Wayne, then calls Batman and never recognizes the identical tone. Later, Batman impersonates Wayne and there's a dummy Wayne involved; and in Tut's final confrontations during the third season, a Batman dummy makes two appearances.

Tut always seems on the verge of uncovering Batman's identity—and when he does, of course, it's literally knocked out of him. Then there's Tut himself. He's Yale Professor of Egyptology William Omaha McElroy. At some point in the past, during a violent student protest, he sustained a concussion that left him believing he was the reincarnation of the boy king, Tutankhamun.

There is clearly a history between King Tut and the Gotham Guardian, since Batman had believed Tut to have died in a warehouse fire the previous year. However, he's back and with a scheme that never quite coalesces in the episode. There's an elaborate scheme to kidnap Bruce Wayne, but to what end never quite makes sense.

The lengthy (for the series) opening begins in Gotham Central Park as an Egyptian statue is placed there by two of Tut's men wearing mummy masks (something the show should have retained as a motif), ruining "the deceptive quiet of the jungle." Once the good citizens get over their amplified horror, Nefertiti's voice is heard proclaiming, "It is written in the stars that on this day shall the great King of the Nile rise up from the tomb and he shall claim his kingdom of Gotham City, and all who oppose him shall be smitten dead."

Word of the sudden arrival of the statue reaches Gordon and Chief O'Hara, who mistakenly refer to it as a Sphinx (possibly the only Egyptian statue the masses at home might be familiar with, although this statue is of a ram-headed god, possibly Khnum). O'Hara suggests it might be a publicity stunt for the new exhibit opening at the Gotham City Museum, and is not once worried about the lack of permitting (how nice it must be to work in Gotham, where such things never come up). Rather than call someone actively engaged in the exhibit, Gordon decides instead to call museum board treasurer Bruce Wayne (because board members are always aware of every aspect of an exhibit).

We cut to stately Wayne Manor, where Bruce, Dick, and Aunt Harriet just happen to be on their way to the very same museum exhibit. Of course, Wayne is confused when Alfred says Gordon wants to speak with him. After confirming the museum had nothing to do with the statue, Wayne determines, "This phenomenon takes on new dimensions... strange and sinister dimensions!" Meanwhile, the commissioner concludes that only the Caped Crusader could investigate the situation. Moments later, Gordon's talking to the same man, and a quick trip to the batpoles gets us into the episode proper.

Once we're in police headquarters, we're told how mild-mannered Professor McElroy had been injured during protests at Yale. What's interesting is that the real-world campus protests of the 1960s are considered part of the decade's later years, so this is almost foreshadowing.

Arriving at the park, Robin exclaims, "Holy hieroglyphics!" while Batman makes the first of many anachronistic conclusions, making viewers doubt his nickname as the "world's greatest detective." He stares at the statue and says it is a "rather good imitation" of the Sphinx at Giza. At least he gets the Fourth Dynasty part right. He doesn't get a chance to correct the nomenclature error before Nefertiti announces, "Whosoever transgresses upon the sacred Sphinx shall be smitten down by Anubis, the jackal god guardian of the cemeteries—and that goes double for Batman."

Let's pause for a history lesson. King Tut is described as King of the Nile, which was not one of Tutankhamun's titles during his brief rule. His leading lady is named Nefertiti, who was actually the wife of Akhenaten, while Tut was Akhenaten's son. (Think about that for a moment.) They're accompanied by a royal scrivener, which sounds cool, but the name is Latin, whereas the real Tut had a royal scribe.

Upon investigation, Robin finds a booby trap, which Batman safely triggers—but one wonders the point of it. Neither hero ponders how the speaker knew the Gotham Guardian was on the scene, but viewers are shown her in a nearby phone booth, using a compact mirror and the sun to signal the Dynamic Duo's arrival to Tut's thugs. She then strolls through the park in full costume, perfectly luring the crimefighters into an ambush. The thugs are run off and the heroes go back to their investigation.

Back in the lair, the scrivener asks, "Why dip that hunk of rock in the park and tip off the suckers to what we're gonna do?!" Tut merely proclaims, "You're a twit." He wants the Dynamic Duo out of his way for the big scheme, whatever it may be, most likely stealing the Egyptian museum's priceless artifacts.

Batman shrugs it off and returns home to change back into Bruce Wayne. Leaving Dick and Harriet at home without explanation, he then conducts a press tour of the Egyptian exhibit. Why is a member of the board on hand, rather than an Egyptologist or curator? Let's not bother with these things. Clearly, this is done to isolate Wayne from everyone. What's nice is that the sole reporter to get any lines in the episode is a black man, one of several such appearances throughout the series, making *Batman* mildly progressive for the era.

When they arrive at the *pièce de résistance*, the sarcophagus of a 3,500-year-old mummy of a 14th-Dynasty king, Wayne intones, "It's a costume of the 14th Dynasty. King Tut's dynasty." Actually, the 14th Dynasty ended in 1650 BC, long before Tut, who was from the 18th Dynasty. The sarcophagus is oddly exposed to the open air.

Worse, Wayne casually opens it and remarks on how well preserved it is when, to the naked eye, it is clearly a fake. The eyes open and there's a collective gasp, with everyone thinking the ancient king has been resurrected. Moreover, they uncover the head and no one, not even Wayne, recognizes Tut.

Handy EMTs arrive, who just happen to be Tut's royal scrivener and vizier. Wisely, Wayne accompanies the precious cargo, only to find himself gassed and kidnapped. If this was the plan all along, what was all that nonsense at the park? Apparently, it was all to set up Nefertiti's next pronouncement (courtesy of cue cards held by Tut): "It was written in the stars and it has come to pass. The great king of the Nile has risen from the sands of time to reclaim his lost kingdom."

Tut takes the mic, announces he has millionaire Bruce Wayne in his grip, and promises a ransom demand while warning off the GCPD and the Dynamic Duo. In the meantime, the two men drive far outside the city limits to a place unknown, with Wayne awakening and discovering his plight. As the ambulance makes a series of hairpin turns, we cut back to a conversation between Gordon and Robin. Gotham's top cop seems more comfortable with adults and insists on speaking with Batman, while Robin can only say he's not available. Upstairs, Harriet is overwhelmed with neither Dick nor Alfred on hand to comfort her. By this point in the series, her kidnapping by Zelda the Great was her only useful appearance, and things would never get better for poor Madge Blake.

The ambulance continues on its interminable ride as Wayne forces his gurney to bang against the poorly secured back door, and he scoots out. Of course, he's headed downhill toward a construction sign warning of a 300-foot drop, and Dozier intones, "Holy cliffhanger!" Interestingly, this is not dissimilar to the fate awaiting Wayne when he was bound, lying down, and heading feet-first in "Fine Feathered Finks."

As the second episode picks up, in true serialized style, we see the same scene, although this time Wayne has managed to free himself from the gurney just before it tumbles over the cliff. The drivers notice nothing.

At Tut's hideaway, everyone's watching a demolition derby until the impatient king changes to the all-day news channel in time to see Gordon and Batman announce that Wayne is safe. Nefertiti proclaims, "Batman! He turns me on!" which earns Tut's ire, but reflects how most of the molls on the series feel about the Caped Crusader. Poor, deluded children. The phrase, a carryover from the Beat Generation, was about to enter the mass populace lexicon thanks to The Beatles' "A Day in the Life."

Let's pause a moment to marvel at the various anachronisms and odd juxtapositions between the past and present. First, we have them watching television. Then there's Nefertiti's diet:

"Nefertiti, you abandoned wench, how many times must I tell you? Queens consume nectar and ambrosia, not hot dogs!" Tut roars.

"So I get hungry—living on nothing but figs and dates and pomegranates," she retorts. "You want a bite?"

"Aaaaah! Unclean!"

But I digress. Batman had saved him not minutes before (the timing of events in this two-parter never makes sense). The Gotham Guardian then announces his intention to take the first airplane to Egypt in order to research at the famed library of Alexandria (establishing that the Batplane does not exist in this reality). Gordon proves he's no smarter than Batman, by assuming he is talking about Alexandria, Virginia. Does this make sense to anyone? Nope, but Tut buys it.

When Nefertiti refers to Tut's alter-ego, he flies into a rage (which comes off as somewhat out of left field) and has her imprisoned by the royal torturers and subjected to "the ancient Theban pebble torture." At this point, one has to wonder where he got all the funds to hire the four comely women who fan him, as well as the thugs, their costumes, the statue, the trucks, and the sizeable lair. Nevertheless, viewers at home appear to be the only ones to wonder such things throughout the series.

While this is happening, Batman reveals his real plan: lulling Tut into attempting to kidnap Wayne once again (an interesting conclusion based on zero evidence). He shoos Harriet away, sending her to the country, then sets up a convincing-looking dummy of the millionaire on the couch. Once Alfred takes the standard-issue universal antidote pill, the plan is set because (as we're told) Egyptian criminals always strike at 6:00—not that the ancient culture counted hours in this manner. Sure enough, a cop arrives bearing a horrible Irish accent (because every cop has to be Irish) and gases Alfred, along with the dummy. As the cop summons help to carry the body, Batman, who has been hiding in plain sight behind a too-thin credenza, makes an acrobatic leap onto the couch and is covered up.

The criminals speed off as Robin begins tracing them via the tracking device in Batman's cowl (without a backup in the utility belt). He notifies Gordon and O'Hara as they are having their evening coffee (Gotham's police never go home or sleep). As the truck drives away, the henchmen, who have previously mocked or questioned Tut's methods, suddenly show wisdom, quoting a proverb and then smiting the blanketed figure. His aim proves true, not only knocking out Batman but also smashing the tracker.

For reasons unknown, Tut is not interested in Batman's identity but instead places him in a giant ceramic jug next to Nefertiti. Some pebble torture has already begun on her, and now Batman must suffer the same fate. Can he reach his utility belt to free himself? Apparently not.

Back at the Batcave, Alfred and Robin deduce Batman's probable whereabouts after the signal was lost and, using the handy Gotham City Plans and Views computer, determine that Tut and company were likely holed up at the Egyptian palace from last year's Gotham City Expo. Now, if they knew that was still in place, why didn't they check that out before anything else happened—say, before the body switcheroo? It would have saved everyone a lot of grief and the police from paying O'Hara overtime.

Speaking of the police, Gordon receives word that Batman can be freed if Bruce Wayne pays a million dollars (no other wealthy people live in Gotham?). Robin says he's on it and convinces Alfred to drive the Batmobile (sans disguise) so the Boy Wonder can save his mentor. As the Batmobile speeds to the Expo grounds, the torture is complete, presumably driving both Nefertiti and Batman insane. (If you consider them reciting "Twinkle, twinkle, little bat, how I wonder where you're at" and laughing together to constitute insanity, then the 1,000-pebble torture must have worked.)

The pair are brought to Tut's throne room, where a crank-up record player starts up, conveniently with a record of "bat music" at the ready, and Tut has the vases cracked apart, commanding the pair to dance. If anything, this feels tacked on, given the popularity of the Batusi just prior to the episodes being shot. Here, we see Batman dance, getting closer to the thugs and punching them out. He then declares his sanity by noting that he kept his mind intact by reciting the multiplication tables backwards. How Nefertiti kept *her* mind intact is never addressed. Instead, there's a sword fight, with Robin arriving to join in the fray. Please note the first use of the "Touché" sound effect.

After subduing the henchmen, Batman and Robin rush after Tut to discover he kayoed Alfred, stole the Batmobile, and is speeding away—a first for the series. The Dynamic Duo gives chase in Tut's truck, only to be hunted by their own vehicle. Batman tries to activate the ejector seat using the Voice-Control Batmobile Relay-Circuit, but of course, that's when the computer decides to glitch. Instead, Tut returns and is about to fire the Bat-Beam and destroy them when the circuit finally connects and he's shot high into the air. He lands, conveniently, on the truck and is rendered unconscious.

Back at Gordon's office, the commissioner apparently has nowhere to lock up the criminal. Therefore, he simply leaves him on the couch, complaining, "The taxpayers are blind to our pleas" for more jail space… as opposed to, say, a psychiatric facility.

Tut awakens and appears to have regained his McElroy persona, completely unaware of where he's been for a year or more. "Whatever will the dean say?" the professor concludes. It won't matter, because Buono struck gold with this part and was brought back early in the second season. The same writers returned for "The Spell of Tut" and "Tut's Case is Shut," which was a rarity for the show, although Stanley Ralph Ross later spoke about how much he loved writing the character as well.

Buono got to play the part in subsequent episodes, practically ad-libbing his entire performance by the third season, making him sound fey, arch, and funny all at the same time. On more than one occasion, Adam West told reporters, "Victor Buono was amazing."

The moll du jour is Ziva Rodann, an Israeli beauty described by the *Canadian Jewish Chronicle* as "the first Israeli actress to be signed to a long-term deal with a major motion picture studio." She affected an appropriate accent, in addition to adding a touch of New York City to her lines, including, "Home, toots, and step on it!" Rodann's acting career would end just three years after this episode aired.

They're surrounded with veteran actors, including Don Barry (as the grand vizier), who was once the lead in the movie serial *The Adventures of Red Ryder*. You can't keep a good thug down, and he's later seen as Tarantula in "Black Widow Strikes Again" and "Caught in the Spider's Den". Dedicated fans will also recognize him from his final role, playing Leonard McCoy's father David in *Star Trek V: The Final Frontier*.

Olan Soule is seen here as the newscaster, but young fans would come to recognize him by his voice alone, as Soule stepped behind the microphone to bring the animated Batman alive in the 1968 Saturday-morning show on CBS, *The Batman/Superman Hour*. He'd continue portraying the Caped Crusader until 1983 and could be heard matching wits with Scooby-Doo or counting on *Sesame Street*. Soule would wind up being replaced by Adam West himself, starting with 1984's *Super Friends: The Legendary Super Powers Show*, though he would shift to playing the Martin Stein half of Firestorm.

Given all the rights issues between Greenway, 20th Century Fox, and DC Comics, it would be decades before King Tut could make the leap to comics. He finally arrived in *Batman Confidential* #26 (2009), by Christina Weir, Nunzio DeFillippis, and the great José Luis García-López. McElroy is here renamed Victor Goodman, a play on Victor Buono ("buono" is Italian for "good"). Earlier, King Tut was shown on *Batman: The Brave and the Bold*, and while he looked like Tut, he had to be renamed the Pharaoh.

While the *Batman* TV show was nonsensical on several levels, we still have to appreciate how it gave us the unforgettable King Tut, who was popular enough to recur when subsequent original foes all failed to gain hold of the audience's interest. Much of that credit goes to Buono, who, at 28, fit right into a world filled with veteran performers dating back to the silent film era. Visually compelling, the Egyptian motif fit perfectly with the colorful world of television's Dynamic Duo.

Robert Greenberger is a writer and editor. A lifelong fan of comic books, comic strips, science fiction and *Star Trek*, he drifted towards writing and editing, encouraged by his father and inspired by Superman's alter ego, Clark Kent.

While at SUNY-Binghamton, Greenberger wrote and edited for the college newspaper, *Pipe Dream*. Upon graduation, he worked for Starlog Press and while there, created *Comics Scene*, the first nationally distributed magazine to focus on comic books, comic strips and animation. In 1984, he joined DC Comics as an Assistant Editor, and went on to be an Editor before moving to Administration as Manager-Editorial Operations. He joined Gist Communications as a Producer before moving to Marvel Comics as its Director-Publishing Operations.

Greenberger rejoined DC in May 2002 as a Senior Editor-Collected Editions. He helped grow that department, introducing new formats and improving the editions' editorial content. In 2006, he joined *Weekly World News* as its Managing Editor until the paper's untimely demise. He then freelanced for an extensive client base including Platinum Studios, scifi.com, DC and Marvel. He helped revitalize *Famous Monsters of Filmland* and served as News Editor at ComicMix.com.

He is a member of the Science Fiction Writers of America and the International Association of Media Tie-In Writers. His novelization of *Hellboy II: The Golden Army* won the IAMTW's Scribe Award in 2009. In 2012, he received his Master of Science in Education from University of Bridgeport and relocated to Maryland where he has taught High School English in Baltimore County. He completed his Master of Arts degree in Creative Writing & Literature for Educators at Fairleigh Dickinson University in 2016.

With others, he cofounded Crazy 8 Press, a digital press hub where he continues to write. His dozens of books, short stories, and essays cover the gamut from young adult nonfiction to original fiction. He's also one of the dozen authors using the penname Rowan Casey to write the Veil Knights urban fantasy series. His most recent works include *100 Greatest Moments* series and editing the forthcoming *Thrilling Adventure Yarns.*

Bob teaches High School English at St. Vincent Pallotti High School in Laurel, MD. He and his wife Deborah reside in Howard County, Maryland. Find him at www.bobgreenberger.com or @bobgreenberger.

ZOWIE!

"Who Else Can Save Us Now?"

"The Bookworm Turns/While Gotham City Burns"
By Paul Kupperberg

Here's some Bat-trivia: The very first surprise "Bat-cameo" took place in the twenty-ninth episode of *Batman*, "The Bookworm Turns," and was made by comedian Jerry Lewis.

The *Batman* cameos survive in popular memory as one of the signature kitsch components of the 1966 hit series, along with the on-screen onomatopoeia of the "Pow! Zap! Bam!" sound effects and the neon bright color palette evocative of the comic book page. There were fourteen of these appearances in all during the show's three seasons, famous faces popping out of whatever window Batman and Robin were passing as they climbed up the side of a building in pursuit of the bad guy of the week.

Most of these pop-up guest stars appeared as themselves, although a few were in costume or character, some to promote other ABC network shows, such as Ted Cassidy, "Lurch" from *The Addams Family*, and Howard Duff as Detective Sam Stone from *Felony Squad*, while others were like Werner Klemperer, who popped his head out in his full Nazi regalia as Colonel Klink from rival CBS series *Hogan's Heroes*. Van Williams and Bruce Lee appeared in their *Green Hornet* and Kato costumes, a program not only on ABC, but also produced by *Batman* showrunner William Dozier.

"[*Batman*] was a show that everyone wanted to do at that period. It was such fun. They were larger-than-life cartoon characters, which are very interesting to play," Roddy McDowall, who appeared as the guest-villain Bookworm in "The Bookworm Turns" and "While Gotham City Burns," told Batman scholar Joel Eisner for his 1986 book, *The Official Batman Batbook*. It was to accommodate all the stars clamoring to appear on television's top show that the Bat-cameo was created. Jerry Lewis, another ABC star and a shrewd self-promoter, lobbied for a spot to promote his own *The Jerry Lewis Show*. The entire Jerry-Batman exchange lasts about fifteen seconds:

Jerry: Are you Batman? Oh, you must be, because that's Robin! Hi, Robin!

Batman: Yes, citizen, but don't be alarmed. We're here on official business!

Jerry: Holy human flies!

Another bit of Bat-trivia: Jerry also had his own DC Comics title at the time, *The Adventures of Jerry Lewis*, which ran for 124 issues between 1952 and 1971. Several superheroes guest-starred with the bumbling Jerry in the mid-1960s, including Superman, Wonder Woman, the Flash, and, of course, Batman (and the Joker) in issue #97 (November-December 1966).

Guest-villain Roddy McDowall began his career in 1938 in his native England when he was nine years old. He appeared in his first U.S. movies after his family moved to Los Angeles in 1941, including in the role of Huw Morgan in John Ford's masterpiece, *How Green Was My Valley*, and alongside fellow child-star Elizabeth Taylor in *Lassie Come Home*.

Unlike earlier bad guys such as the Riddler, Joker, and Penguin, Bookworm was created for the show (and wouldn't appear in a comic book until 1989) by writer Rik Vallaerts, who told Joel Eisner, "It was very hard to make a presentation to the producers, because they didn't really know what they were going to do.... The only thing that I did that was even partially different was to develop an intelligent super-criminal. I had a hell of a hard time trying to sell it because the number of people who read books in Hollywood is rather limited."

All of Batman's rouges had a schtick. Bookworm's was books and literature. He wore a suit and a hat (with a built-in reading lamp) that were supposed to be leather bookbinding but were made out of vinyl plastic, and an oversized pair of thick, radio-equipped, black-framed glasses. Bookworm is, by his own admission, a failed novelist who uses his vast knowledge of literature to plan and execute crimes based on famous books and quotations. He is assisted by the voluptuous Lydia Limpet, and henchmen dressed in printer's aprons and hats made of folded book pages with names like Printer's Devil, Pressman, and Typesetter.

Superhero TV shows and movies, like comic books, depend on the viewer's/reader's willing suspension of disbelief. Viewers accept that millionaire playboy Bruce Wayne is secretly Batman and, despite most of his actions to the contrary in this two-parter, that this Batman is the "world's greatest detective."

The ten-year-old who first saw these episodes in 1966 believed that to be true. For the sixty-plus-year-old looking back on them, an extra helping of suspension of disbelief—along with a softening dash of nostalgia—is necessary.

Part One opens at stately Wayne Manor, where Bruce Wayne and Dick Grayson are watching the televised ribbon-cutting ceremony for the opening of Gotham City's new Amerigo Columbus Bridge, when Dick spots Bookworm passing through the crowd.

Bookworm radios henchman Printer's Devil, who is waiting with a rifle on the roof of a van, ordering him to "Start chapter one!" A moment later, Police Commissioner Gordon is shot and plummets from the bridge to the water below. Aunt Harriet summons up the thought of all Gothamites when she says she hopes Batman and Robin were watching,

"Who else can save us now?" she cries.

Who, indeed?! Bruce and Dick hit the Bat-poles and, moments later, the Dynamic Duo is Gotham City (14 Miles!) bound. Leaving the Batmobile outside Police Headquarters, they race inside. As soon as they're gone, Bookworm's moll, Lydia Limpet, saunters by and drops a hardcover copy of *For Whom the Bell Tolls*, by Ernest Hemingway, into the car.

Reaching Gordon's office, Batman and Robin are as surprised as the grieving Chief O'Hara when an indignant Commissioner Gordon comes huffing in ("Holy reincarnation!" cries Robin), angry over having missed the ribbon-cutting because of being arrested by a "monumentally stupid" officer named A.S. Scarlet, badge number 1887, for overdue parking. Chief O'Hara says there is no badge number 1887 on the force, but Batman has the answer: Sir Arthur Conan Doyle's first Sherlock Holmes story was "A Study in Scarlet," which was published in 1887. "A typical twisted Bookworm joke!" Robin over-emotes.

They are interrupted by the beeping Batmobile's Bat-bomb detector in Batman's utility belt. Batman activates the ejector seat by remote control, catapulting the book into the air, where it harmlessly ("Holy explosion!") explodes. Printer's Devil, planted as a lookout eating his lunch on the steps of police headquarters, radios Bookworm that "Plot A" has failed, but that "Plot B" is "still up in the air." A moment later, Batman and Robin race back outside where they (a) find the cover from the exploded book, and (b) engage in a brief conversation with Printer's Devil.[6]

(A) provides the duo with no immediate clues, but (b) injects a level of cluelessness that is only the episode's first hint that the

[6] *As originally scripted, there was a part-two callback to the fake assassination as Printer's Devil supposedly guns down Bookworm and the rest of the gang to divert Batman's and Robin's attention and allow them to ambush the unsuspecting heroes from behind. That scene, according to Eisner, was cut for being too gruesome, leaving that plot point dangling in the wind.*

Dark Knight Detective might not be as smart as advertised. Despite Printer Devil's obvious henchmen garb of apron and folded paper hat, and knowing who it is they are up against, Batman doesn't give the bad guy a second glance.

Back at the Batcave, their examination of the book shows the clue to be nothing more than what it looks like, according to the frustrated Robin: "A perfectly ordinary asbestos book cover." Batman insists it must mean something because Bookworm "prepares every super-crime like the frustrated novelist he is. Every page, every chapter, is an integral part of one stolen plot. Even that charade at the bridge this morning… Great heavens! Of course, the bridge!" Suddenly, it all falls into place as Batman remembers that the plot of *For Whom the Bell Tolls* concerns the hero's mission to *blow up a bridge*! "Holy detonator!" says Robin.

At his book-stuffed hideout, Bookworm refuses to reveal his planned "super-crime" to his henchmen, but he waxes poetic about his love for books and brags that he has memorized the plot of every story ever published. Lydia makes the mistake of wondering aloud why, "with a mind like yours, you don't write your own bestseller?" Bookworm explodes, accusing her of mocking him because, "I have no originality…I am a master of stolen plots!" When he finally calms down, Bookworm reveals that "it is time for us to put a little twist into our plot."

And so, that night, Commissioner Gordon sends Batman and Robin to investigate a "strange occurrence" at a warehouse that "involves a bridge." They arrive to find a giant-sized image of the Amerigo Columbus Bridge projected on a wall. "Holy magic lantern! An immense picture of the new bridge!" Batman explains, "[Bookworm's] blown it up all right… that photograph of the bridge is hugely enlarged, *blown up* in photographer's lingo."

The duo climb the wall of the warehouse (meeting Jerry Lewis along the way) to gain the high ground to search for the source of the projected picture (which is a projector mounted atop Bookworm's Bookmobile van). Here, again, the viewer might wonder about Batman's much-heralded forensic and deductive abilities. Absent any hint or mention of mirrors or tricks to divert or reroute the path of the projected image, physics demands that the projector be in a pretty much direct, unobscured line of sight from the image it's projecting. In other words: the projector had to be *right behind them*! Instead, they climb the building to find the Bookmobile in an alley, then do a "reverse Bat-climb," and drive to its location in the Batmobile.

"Odd. An abandoned Bookmobile," Batman muses.

"Could it really be one from the Gotham City Public Library?" Robin asks.

"I doubt it, Robin. Not with that photo-projector built into the roof. I doubt whether it's entirely abandoned either," Batman says.

Once again, they show no trace of a lawman's instinct. They stand, fully exposed to whatever trap Bookworm might launch, calmly deploying the Ultrasonic Bat-ray to hit the other vehicle with 12,000 decibels of sound, driving the villain and his henchmen from hiding. There's a brief fight (but only after Batman reminds his opponents to take off their glasses, telling Robin, "Remember, never hit a man with glasses!") and after a few "Pow! Biff! Socks!" the bad guys escape down a previously prepared escape hole. The heroes are left to wonder the purpose of Bookworm luring them there. The answer to that is back in the Bookmobile: the bound and gagged Lydia Limpet. In a long overdue display of common sense, Batman deduces this could be a set-up, that she could be a member of the gang planted there to feed them false information.

Then, in a gross denial of Lydia's civil rights even for 1966, the year of the Miranda Decision, Batman hits her with a knock-out spray and takes her to the Batcave, where she is hooked to the Hypermetric Lie-Detector for interrogation while still in her drugged sleep. She tells them her name and that she works for Bookworm, but the only information she has on the criminal's scheme is that it requires Batman and Robin to die.

When she comes to, Lydia is back in the Bookmobile, unaware she'd made a full, if drugged confession. She plays her part, claiming to have overheard Bookworm's scheme; he plans to steal the original

Declaration of Independence from Independence Hall. "He strikes at midnight," she says.

Batman leaves Robin with Lydia and heads to Independence Hall, knowing he's walking into a trap. Robin, while not sucker enough to untie her as she sweetly asks, does acquiesce to Lydia's request that he read to her while they wait for the authorities to arrive. She asks for "that fourth [book] from the end of the shelf." Every bit on the ball as his mentor, he plucks the book from the shelf without question. He glances at the title, saying balefully, "*Complete English History*? This kind of stuff always puts me to sleep." Quite literally in this case, as a plume of gas erupts in his face as soon as he opens the cover and knocks him unconscious. Obviously smarter than her opponents, Lydia had realized the Dynamic Duo were on to her because they kept calling her "Miss Limpet," even though she'd never told them her name. She radios a warning to Bookworm.

Robin comes to and finds himself tied upside down to the clapper of Big Benjamin, the massive bell in the Wayne Memorial Clock Tower (named, oh irony of ironies, "in honor of Bruce Wayne's father"). There, in only one minute, at the stroke of midnight, he will be bashed to death when, as Bookworm reminds him, he will learn that the answer to *For Whom the Bell Tolls* is "This bell tolls for *thee*!"

"Holy headaches!" Robin declares, after the gang has left him to swing in the episode's cliffhanger.

Meanwhile, we learn, as part two opens the following night, that while Robin was being strung up, Batman had arrived at Independence Hall, where Chief O'Hara (to whom he had radioed ahead for back-up) informed him that a search had failed to turn up any sign of Bookworm. They also couldn't find Robin or the Bookmobile in that alley Batman had sent them to. When Robin failed to answer Batman's call on the Utility-belt Frequency, the Caped Crusader hadn't panicked. Instead, he'd put himself into some weird fugue state, "trying to fathom the subconscious of a deadly criminal." This pulls up bits of earlier dialog, which all lead him to conclude (out of plot convenience more than any actual deductive reasoning) that the Hemingway book title and Lydia's warning that "*he* strikes at midnight" all point to Robin being tied up in the bell in the Wayne Memorial Clock Tower... because it is the "one clock in Gotham City that is called '*he*!'"

Batman and Chief O'Hara race to the clock tower, arriving "mere seconds" before midnight. O'Hara tries shooting out the clockworks, and when that fails, Batman breaks out the Batzooka to fire grappling hooks at the tower and the hands of the clock. Attaching those lines to the positive charge of the Batmobile's nuclear power source, he revs up the power turbine and tells O'Hara to "pray that the clapper and the bell will be positively charged and thus repel each other!"

Spoiler alert: They do.

Though frustrated by his failure to smear Robin, Bookworm is philosophical. "Facts are stubborn things," he quotes, and the fact is, "our bats have flown the belfry, unaccountably still squeaking." But Bookworm's "brain-drenched mind" has devised a new plot twist to salvage their super-crime in waiting.

The next day, Bookworm knocks on the door of Wayne Manor, claiming to be from the Library Bookmobile, gases Aunt Harriet and Alfred, and steals a "priceless cookbook" from Bruce's collection. Batman and Robin are downstairs in the Batcave the entire time, but it takes a Bat-phone call from Commissioner Gordon to learn that their own home has been robbed. The commissioner also tells them that a giant cookbook has suddenly appeared on a Gotham City street corner.

Forgoing concern for family for the public good, the duo speed back into Gotham City to check out the giant edition of *The Delight of Cooking*. A scan with the Batmobile's high-energy radar confirms that the massive tome is hollow and that the cover can be safely opened using their Superpowered Bat-magnet.

Bookworm and Lydia are watching from a nearby rooftop, the leather-bound criminal confident that the Dynamic Duo will walk into his trap because, "in the words of the poet, 'curiosity killed the bat.'"

And, once again showing no caution or judgment whatsoever,

the Dynamic Duo step inside, which is set up like a quaint, old-fashioned kitchen, complete with a pot of soup bubbling on the stove. There is no attempt to prevent the door from being closed on them, no check for traps or explosives. Robin even goes so far as to taste the soup, which is Bookworm's cue to slam shut the book via remote control and trap them as the interior fills with superheated steam. Before leaving the heroes to boil to death, Bookworm taunts them with the fact that their deaths finally leave him free to commit his super-crime… for which he needs the Batmobile!

Fortunately, Bookworm's trap doesn't prevent Batman from radioing Alfred in the Batcave ("It's his regular time for dusting the atomic pile," Batman knows) and putting the Bat Anti-Crime Computer through its paces. By the time Gordon and the cops blow the book open, Batman and Robin are gone. "Consumed, I fear," the grief-stricken Gordon irrationally exclaims. "Totally consumed in this diabolical Hell's kitchen!"

Meanwhile, in an alley behind Gotham City's Morganbilt Library (an "unparalleled repository of literary treasures"), Bookworm has the gang gathered around the Batmobile, studying plans to the library. The giant book and the robbery at Wayne Manor were just diversions to draw out Batman and Robin so Bookworm can kill them and steal the Batmobile. Now he tells them, in a hushed tone, "Directly ahead, through that wall, is the air-conditioned vault containing treasures beyond imagination." This includes seven Gutenberg Bibles and eleven Shakespeare First Folios, but all are barricaded behind an impenetrable three feet of cement and eighteen inches of steel.

Impenetrable that is, except to the Batmobile's Bat-beam, which effortlessly blasts a hole in the wall. But before the gang can go in to claim their loot, Batman and Robin step out into the alley. Alfred's computer search had located the manhole cover under the stove through which the steam was being piped. They had escaped underground and had headed straight to the Morganbilt, because the microphone in the stolen Batmobile had recorded and relayed to the Batcave Bookworm's gloating recitation of his plans during the drive to the library with Lydia.

The rest is another round of "Pow! Bam! Biff!" before the inevitable takedown, and, as they're slapping the Bat-cuffs on Lydia, Batman reminds her, "The oldest plot is still the best. Crime does not pay."

Neither, in the long run, does dissecting the story for logic or, well, story.

Though dressed up with a campy attitude and a few winks and nods to the grown-ups, *Batman* was still essentially a cartoon. Fans might have preferred a more serious approach, but ABC signaled its feelings about the property from the start by assigning it to William Dozier, a sitcom producer who was also famously embarrassed by the comic book origin of the source material.

In 2016, Warner Bros released the animated feature *Batman: Return of the Caped Crusaders*, made in the style and milieu of *Batman '66*. It "starred" the voices of the then surviving members of the cast: Adam "Batman" Adam West (who died in 2017), Burt "Robin" Ward, and Julie "Catwoman" Newmar. The story and tone of the animated iteration wouldn't have been out of place in the live-action original; if anything, portraying that cartoon sensibility in an actual cartoon softened the absurdity and campiness.

Still, even in cartoon or sitcom terms, Bookworm's turn on *Batman* is riddled with logic and plot holes and padded with filler to show off the "Bat-this" and "Bat-that" gimmick, pandering to an audience of adolescent expectations. Everything in the story is made to seem bigger and more important than it is: Bookworm's big "super-crime" is to steal the Batmobile so he can use it to rob some old books from a library, a goal puffed up by Bookworm's mysterious attitude and murderous intent. It was a given that Batman's villains would follow their compulsions to commit colorful and entertaining crimes, but the need to be entertained always overwhelmed the needs of a logical story. Bookworm's efforts are all aimed at drawing Batman and the Batmobile out into the open so he can steal it. The giant cookbook was sure to accomplish that, leaving Bookworm's book theft at Wayne Manor to seem like some random, unrelated incident, maybe just an excuse to give Aunt Harriet and Alfred a few moments' more airtime. Why was every part of the scheme so overblown and complicated? And, of course, overshadowing any other story drivers was the inevitable cliffhanger deathtrap, one viewers knew was doomed to failure (usually by some cheat in the storytelling) even before the narrator finished inviting us back tomorrow night, "same Bat-time, same Bat-channel!"

In the end, none of that mattered. Viewers were tuning in precisely for those exaggerations and over-the-top moments of silliness.

In retrospect, Jerry Lewis was the appropriate star to make the inaugural Bat-cameo. He was as much a human cartoon as Adam West's Caped Crusader, and his wide-eyed, mugging nine-year-old persona was a perfect fit for *Batman*, whose core audience, at least in terms of creative sensibilities, was in the same demographic.

Taken at face value from these episodes, Batman himself is little more than a stuffy, moralizing dunce who wouldn't recognize a clue if it were chewing on his leg. He is more of a Jacques Clouseau than a Sherlock Holmes. It's largely our fondness for the character and the subtle wink behind the mask that lets us accept this parody in spandex as the "world's greatest detective."

Thank goodness for nostalgia.

Paul Kupperberg is a forty-plus-year veteran comic book writer. He has written Batman in many forms, from comics to prose stories to storybooks, and hundreds of other characters ranging from Archie to Zatanna in more than one thousand comic book stories. Paul has also been an editor for DC Comics, *Weekly World News*, and *WWE Kids Magazine*, and is currently publishing through Crazy 8 Press (Crazy8Press.com) and Charlton Neo Comics (morttodd.com/Charlton), publishers of *Paul Kupperberg's Guide to Writing Comic Books*. You can follow him on Facebook, Twitter, and Instagram, and at PaulKupperberg.com.

ZOK!

Riddles in Silence

"Death in Slow Motion/The Riddler's False Notion"

By Peter Sanderson

One reason that the first season of the *Batman* TV show is the best is that it took both villains and plots from the *Batman* comics. The final example of this in season one was the two-parter "Death in Slow Motion" and "The Riddler's False Notion," directed by Charles R. Rondeau and written by Dick Carr, which was based on "The Joker's Comedy Capers," written by John Broome and drawn by Carmine Infantino, in *Detective Comics* issue #347 (1965). But that statement leads to the obvious question: Why did the TV show transform a Joker story into a Riddler story?

In the comic book version, the Joker conceives a scheme to create a new silent comedy movie for a wealthy silent film aficionado by the unlikely name of Cornelius Van Van. The Joker's ultimate goal is to gain access to Van Van's mansion and rob him. So the Joker perpetrates a series of robberies while disguised as various famous silent comedians, performing gags in the process, while his henchmen capture it all on film. This certainly is appropriate for the Joker in his "Clown Prince of Crime" period in the 1960s, before he turned into the insane serial killer that has been familiar in comics and movies from the 1970s onward. The Joker prides himself on his comic abilities, and stories have established that he admires the great comedians of the past. But it doesn't fit the Riddler's modus operandi of puzzles and conundrums.

Perhaps for legal reasons, the comic did not use the actual names of the real-life comedians whom the Joker impersonated. In 1965, when the comic was published, Charlie Chaplin, Buster Keaton, and Harold Lloyd were all still alive; Keaton died in February 1965, months before these episodes first aired. So the comic substitutes other names for the comedians that the Joker imitates: "The Tramp" (Chaplin), "Deadpan" (Keaton), "Specs" (Lloyd), "Cross-Eyes" (Ben Turpin), and "Banjo" (Harpo Marx). Harpo did not appear in silent films, but he famously was always mute in the talkies he made with his brothers. By coincidence or not, the character based on Harpo Marx in George S. Kaufman and Moss Hart's classic stage comedy *The Man Who Came to Dinner* was also called Banjo. Carmine Infantino brilliantly depicted the likenesses of all these comedy stars, making it clear who they were supposed to be.

So why substitute the Riddler for the Joker? It was probably due to the practical considerations of adapting this comic to live action. How hard would it be to make an actor look like all of these different people? Besides, the actor in question would have to be capable of imitating them. Despite his long, successful acting career, Cesar Romero, who played the Joker on the TV series, was not known for impersonating real people or as a comedian.

In contrast, Frank Gorshin, who played the Riddler, had previously been most famous as an impressionist on television and in night clubs. In fact, his repertoire included the actor Richard Widmark, and Gorshin's famous Riddler laugh seems like a more elaborate version of Widmark's eerie giggle in his breakout role as a psychotic killer in the 1947 movie *Kiss of Death*. So Gorshin was a good choice to impersonate Chaplin as the Little Tramp, as he does in the opening of the first episode. He is good at it, too, aside from relying overly much on Chaplin's mannerism of tipping his hat.

Writer Dick Carr's early draft of the teleplay also has the Riddler impersonating Keaton and Lloyd in the course of the story, but he does neither in the actual episodes. The show makes up and costumes Gorshin to look reasonably like Chaplin, but perhaps it was decided that it was too difficult to make him look like Keaton and Lloyd. Perhaps, too, the makers of the show reasoned that the largely young audience for the show wouldn't know who either Keaton or Lloyd were, though Chaplin's image as the Little Tramp was probably still universally recognized. And there may have been legal reasons for not impersonating Keaton and Lloyd on screen.

However, Keaton and Lloyd are still referenced in the TV show. Solving one of the Riddler's riddles, Batman comes up with the word "deadpan," as in deadpan humor, doing or saying funny things with a straight face. (Of course, that is one of Adam West's strengths in performing Batman.) This is also the name that the comic had given the Buster Keaton character. Later, when the Riddler tries to push Robin off the ledge of a tall building, both Batman and narrator Desmond Doomsday openly refer to Harold Lloyd, who was most famous for dangling on the side of a building high above the street in the silent comedy *Safety Last!* Note, by the way, that although the Riddler speaks of "the immortal Charlie," the name "Chaplin" is never uttered. Would that, on top of visually referencing the Tramp, have been crossing a legal line?

So instead of having the Riddler pose as various silent comedians, the makers of the show broadened the theme of the story from silent comedy to silent movies in general, giving them a wider range of material to evoke. Indeed, these two episodes are filled with allusions to the silent movie era.

The most impressive of these is casting Francis X. Bushman as the wealthy silent movie buff, whose name has been changed from Cornelius Van Van to Mr. Van Jones. Bushman had appeared in hundreds of silent films, but he is best remembered for playing the villain Messala in the 1924 version of *Ben-Hur*. Bushman is an iconic figure in that film as he competes against Ben-Hur in the famous chariot race, wearing a winged helmet. These *Batman* episodes were Bushman's final screen appearances, as he died later in 1966.

Neil Hamilton, who played Commissioner Gordon, had also worked in silent films. He and Bushman did a silent movie together, *The Grip of the Yukon* (1928), so it is appropriate that they share a scene on *Batman*.

The Riddler ultimately steals Mr. Van Jones's rare print of a silent movie called *The Great Train Hold-up*. This is an obvious reference to a real-life early silent movie, *The Great Train Robbery*, from 1904. But *The Great Train Robbery* is hardly rare: You can easily find it on YouTube nowadays. In the final act of "The Riddler's False Notion," the Riddler dons a large mustache and a cowboy outfit. Perhaps intentionally, the Riddler is thus made to look like the most recognizable character in The *Great Train Robbery*, the outlaw who fires a gun at the camera in close-up.

The Riddler's film director is named Von Bloheim, an allusion to Erich Von Stroheim, one of the great directors of the silent era, whose films include *Greed*, which survives in severely edited form. Von Stroheim was also renowned as an actor, "The Man You Love to Hate," for his villainous roles. But he is best known today for playing the German prison camp commandant in Jean Renoir's *Grand Illusion* and the butler in Billy Wilder's *Sunset Boulevard*, neither of whom were villains. Von Bloheim was played by Theo Marcuse, a prolific actor in 1960s television who died too young. Two of his other memorable roles were as Korob, one of the alien sorcerers in the *Star Trek* episode "Catspaw" and as the dictatorial Devil's Island prison commandant in *The Wild Wild West* episode "The Night of the Bottomless Pit."

The Riddler's cameraman is called "C. B.," an allusion to Cecil B. DeMille, who had directed both silent films and talkies, and was known for his spectacular epics set in ancient Rome or recounting stories from the Bible. DeMille directed both the silent and sound versions of *The Ten Commandments*. In the comic, the Joker poses as "Mr. DeNil" to make the deal to film the silent movie: the name seems to combine "DeMille" with the Devil.

The Riddler's female assistant, played by Sherry Jackson, is named Pauline, after the heroine of the 1914 movie serial *The Perils of Pauline*. Oddly, this character has no name in Carr's early script for these *Batman* episodes, though the name Pauline seems such an obvious choice. Jackson started out as a child actress in movies and television, most notably in comedian Danny Thomas's TV sitcom *Make Room for Daddy*, as Baby Boomers may recall from their childhood. Those Boomers were probably startled when Jackson reemerged as a strikingly sexy adult in 1960s television series, notably in the aptly titled *Star Trek* episode "What Are Little Girls Made Of?" In "Death in Slow Motion" Jackson as Pauline poses at one point as an impoverished waif wearing a tattered dress. Paulette Goddard's ragged dress in Chaplin's *Modern Times* is analogous. But silent movie heroines did not usually wear anything as revealing as Pauline's dress, which bares her entire legs. This really seems to be a reminder that *Batman* was filmed in the mid-1960s, so the show was effectively putting her in a micro-minidress to memorable effect. (Real miniskirts did not appear on the show until the Penguin's campaign girls turned up in the second season's "Hizzoner the Penguin.") Sherry Jackson is one of the few prominent actors from the *Batman* TV show who is still with us.

"The Perils of Pauline" serial is associated in the popular imagination with cliffhangers. In actuality, Pauline was freed from each of her perils by the end of each episode. Still, it should be pointed out that the *Batman* TV show, as long as it aired two-parters, carried on the movie serials' tradition of cliffhangers, and that Batman's first screen appearances had been in movie serials. And, of course, "Desmond Doomsday's" narration of *Batman* TV episodes (actually performed by executive producer William Dozier) derives from radio serials.

Viewers might also be interested to know that the theater manager in the opening of "Death in Slow Motion" was played by Walter Woolf King, who was not a veteran of silent films but did appear in early talkies, and is best remembered as the villainous singer in the Marx Brothers' classic *A Night at the Opera* (1935). Was his appearance in this *Batman* episode a coincidence or an intentional allusion to early movie comedy?

The cliffhanger in these Riddler episodes has Robin about to be split in two by a spinning sawmill blade. This, too, is a famous silent movie melodrama trope. Although the popular image is of a woman endangered in a sawmill, the most popular use of this trope in the silent era was in the 1917 film *Blue Jeans*, in which a woman rescues her husband from the sawmill blade.

Pauline and her mini-dress are involved with the pie fight that the Riddler stages, continuing the comics theme of staging crimes in the style of silent comedy. Of course, the pie fight is an archetypal silent and slapstick comedy trope. Apparently, it originated onstage and was used by Fred Karno's British vaudeville troupe, whose performers included Charlie Chaplin and Stan Laurel. The first pie fight on film was in Ben Turpin's *Mr. Flip* in 1909. Producer Mack Sennett used pie fights in his comedies, and Chaplin put one in his short *Behind the Screen* in 1916. The greatest pie fight in the silent era was in Laurel and Hardy's *The Second Hundred Years* (1927). *The Three Stooges* had their first onscreen pie fight in *In the Sweet Pie and Pie* (1941). The most spectacular pie fight in the sound era is in director Blake Edwards' *The Great Race*, which came out in 1965, only a year before these *Batman* episodes. Pie throwing has remained an enduring trope, used by comedians ranging from Soupy Sales to Monty Python (in their stage show). And the Tramp shoots pies out of a cannon at people in *The Joker's Comedy Capers*, the source for these Riddler episodes.

At the start of "The Riddler's False Notion," the Riddler taunts Batman while dressed in what is popularly thought of as the traditional costume of a silent movie melodrama villain: top hat, cape, handlebar mustache, and whip. This image derives from Victorian stage melodramas. The whip may be an allusion to Simon Legree, the racist villain of the novel *Uncle Tom's Cabin*, which was adapted for the stage. But by the silent movie era, this stereotypical image had already become old hat. The image has survived mainly through parodies of the popular conception of old-time movie villains. Examples include Willie Wormwood in E. C. Segar's *Thimble Theatre* comic strip, Oil Can Harry in *Mighty Mouse* cartoons, Snidely Whiplash in *Dudley Do-Right* cartoons, the Hooded Claw in Hanna-Barbera's *The Perils of Penelope Pitstop*" (a direct parody of the premise of "The Perils of Pauline"), and Professor Fate in director Blake Edwards' *The Great Race*.

In the opening of "Death in Slow Motion," we see an excerpt of an actual silent comedy film featuring the Keystone Kops. These characters are also still associated with silent comedy a century later. A band of comically incompetent policeman who plunge any situation into slapstick chaos, they appeared in the early silent comedies made by producer Mack Sennett at his Keystone film company (where Chaplin got his start in movies). This film is supposedly being shown at Gotham City's Washington Center, a blatant allusion to New York City's Lincoln Center performing arts college; both are named after Presidents. Lincoln Center was still quite new when this episode debuted in the spring of 1966. Its first building had opened in 1962 and its central building, the new Metropolitan Opera House, would not open until the fall of 1966, months after this episode was first shown. Gotham City has always been a fictionalized version of New York City, and the TV show made the parallels clear through parodic names like this.

Not every sequence in this *Batman* two-parter seems to have a specific parallel in silent movies. The Riddler spikes the lemonade at Mr. Van Jones's temperance party with a drug that makes the attendees start fighting each other. The resulting melee is chaotic rather than funny, and there seems to be no famous en masse fight scene in actual silent comedies that does not involve pies. Meanwhile, Pauline goes to Robin while wearing a Little Bo Peep costume, complete with shepherd's crook. Even by the often-absurd standards of this series, it seems hard to believe that Robin seems to accept her costume as normal streetwear, yet she is easily able to gas and capture him. Her costume may be intended to evoke the innocent heroines of silent film, much like her tattered minidress, but it comes from nursery rhymes, not silent movies. And when Batman and Robin are knocked down by a gigantic book on silent film, that seems to be a leftover gag from the Bookworm episodes.

What is most surprising about these episodes is that they give a look into the darker side of Adam West's "light knight." Like the Bookworm episodes, these provide an unusual case of Robin being the sole victim of the cliffhanger death trap and Batman trying to rescue him. After Pauline captures Robin, the Riddler ties him up to be split in half by the aforementioned sawmill blade. As usual, when the villain captures a member of the Dynamic Duo on this show, he may attempt to kill him but it never occurs to the villain to unmask him. (the Joker, during his first appearance on the series, is an exception.)

By the way, with the Riddler claiming he is going to make a "double" of Robin with this death trap stunt, this might have been an even more appropriate tactic for Two-Face to employ if the producers had used him. Batman arrives at the scene of the crime but, to his horror, witnesses the saw bisect "Robin," only to realize nearly instantly that it was actually a mannequin. Still, the fact that he witnessed Robin's apparent death, coupled with the knowledge that the real Robin is still in danger, infuriates Batman. Seeing Pauline nearby, he angrily orders her to surrender, saying he might resort to violence if she doesn't. This is shocking in the context of the *Batman* TV series, in which Batman usually seems so calm and which, after all, was intended by its creators as a comedy[7]. Subsequently, Batman takes Pauline to the Batcave to interrogate her, bringing Commissioner Gordon along as a witness to ensure that he does not step over any legal line. (Both are rendered unconscious by sleeping gas during the journeys back and forth to make sur they do not know the Batcave's location.)

This Batcave sequence is not in Carr's original teleplay, so it is unclear whether he or someone else added it, or why. But it proves to be a big deal for Gordon, who is thrilled to see the Batcave at last. Gordon seems to be Batman's biggest fan. But he is also Batman's

[7] *Though he does furiously threaten to kill the villains in* Batman: The Movie, *discussed elsewhere in this volume.*

enabler. Is Batman really acting legally here? He analyzes Pauline's breath to determine whether or not she is telling the truth. But is he arguably compelling her to testify against herself, violating the Fifth Amendment? He and Gordon had intimidated her before the questioning by informing her that there have been people who came to the Batcave "who never left." Could this possibly be a reference to Molly's demise in the first Riddler two-parter, or to the fate of the Penguin's minions who disintegrate in the Batcave as a result of an unintended accident in the *Batman* movie that came out months later in 1966? (Quite possibly, the screenplay was already written when these Riddler episodes were shot.)

Strangely, the Riddler does not seem to react to Pauline's capture, and Batman rescues Robin from being pushed off a building. But Batman's anger and his use of questionable methods seem to suggest that even in a light-hearted comedy series like this, the Caped Crusader's nature as a dark, driven vigilante sometimes reemerges. Batman's rage and desperation to save Robin also indicate the depth of his fatherly, protective feeling for his ward.

If you think about it, the Riddler's plot in these episodes doesn't make much sense. In the opening, Mr. Van Jones witnesses the Riddler's Chaplin impersonation, but whereas the other bystanders find it hilarious, Van Jones is outraged at what he sees as an amateurish attempt to imitate a comedy great. So why would he find the Riddler's other silent comedy crimes funny? How could the Riddler capture all the camera angles of these crimes in his film when he had only one cameraman? (In the early version of the script, the Riddler actually complains about this.) And how could the Riddler have knitted all these disparate scenes he filmed into a coherent movie? Was Van Jones so oblivious that he did not recognize the sequences in the film as showing actual crimes that were surely reported in the press? After all, one of them was the big fight at his own party! But then, in the final act, Van Jones addresses the filmmaker as "Mr. Riddler." So either he somehow doesn't know about this infamous criminal or he was willing to employ a super-villain while naïvely never expecting to become his target.

It is rather odd that "The Joker's Comedy Capers" in the comic and the Riddler TV episodes based on that story took silent movies as their theme. The kids who comprised virtually all of the comics' readership at the time, and who made up much of the TV show's viewership, would not have any familiarity with silent movies. The silent movie era had ended nearly four decades before 1966, so some adults in their early 40s might be unfamiliar with silent comedy movies. Probably, Julius Schwartz and Gardner Fox in the comics knew silent comedies from their own childhood and did the silent movie theme to amuse themselves. The makers of the *Batman* TV show may have felt the same way, but they made sure to draw on images from silent movies that had persisted in the popular imagination. Note that in the original comic book, Schwartz did not spotlight the silent movie theme on the cover, surely realizing how little it would mean in inducing kids to buy the issue. Reportedly, Schwartz often came up with a cover idea first and then assigned one of his writers to concoct a story around it. If that happened in this case, then Schwartz and Fox devised a story that really had nothing to do with the cover, aside from using the Joker, but that appealed to their presumed nostalgia for silent comedy, and then found a way to fit the cover scene into their story.

It is interesting to consider what the TV show left out in adapting "The Joker's Comedy Capers." The cover for that issue features the eerie, disturbing sight of Carmine Infantino's macabre version of the Joker wearing a Batman costume. When the Joker stages his crime disguised as Chaplin, he fights two henchmen posing as Batman and Robin. The Joker is a trickster character, and disguises and figurative or literal shapeshifting are appropriate for him. "The Joker's Comedy Capers" even refers to the Joker as "that man of a thousand false fronts." Of course, in the course of the comics story, the Joker also impersonates five real comedians and even disguises himself to look like an archetypal old-school film director as Mr. DeNil. So this story seems to have a secondary theme of doubling and disguise. This aspect turns up in the TV adaptation as well, through the Riddler's Chaplin impersonation, through Pauline's various guides, and through the Riddler's mannequin that serves as a Robin double.

A highlight of the comics story is when the Joker tries to steal the Batmobile but is thwarted by its alarm and security system. This doesn't happen in these Riddler episodes. However, there is a similar scene in the Mad Hatter episodes earlier that season. Perhaps the series' writers had spotted the attempted Batmobile theft in the Joker story and transplanted it to their Mad Hatter episodes instead.

What most makes "Death in Slow Motion" and "The Riddler's False Notion" memorable episodes is Frank Gorshin's performance. Of all the Riddler two-parters in the first season, all of which are strong, this is arguably the best. It should be remembered that in the comics, the Riddler was an obscure costumed villain who had only appeared twice in the 1940s. Editor Julius Schwartz and writer Gardner Fox had revived him in 1964 in the comics, and their story was clearly one of those that the show's executive producer, William Dozier, and head writer, Lorenzo Semple, Jr., read in researching Batman. (The Molehill Mob, from Gardner Fox's first Riddler story, turn up in the show's first Riddler episodes, in fact.) Dozier and Semple were obviously taken with the character, and they made him the villain in the first episodes of the TV series, rather than the more well-known Joker or Penguin.

It was Gorshin's indelible performance that elevated the Riddler to the status of A-list *Batman* villain. Keep in mind that Gorshin, Romero, Burgess Meredith, and other "special guest villains" in 1966 were creating the way of playing comic book costumed supervillains, something that no one had done before, finding a viable combination of being believably sinister and menacing while still being funny and appealing. Perhaps still inspired by Richard Widmark, Gorshin came across as a credible, formidable underworld boss when wearing the question mark-themed suit that the show created (and which was not from the comics, although later comics and films adapted it). Gorshin's Riddler took a manic glee in his crimes, evident both through his distinctive laugh and his hyperactive body movements. But he would also frequently stop and become quiet, as he considered his next move, creating the impression of a sinister, brilliant craftiness. Especially good are Gorshin's reactions when he thinks he may finally have destroyed Batman: He obviously finds it hard to believe that he finally succeeded. He does not have a moment like that in this two-parter, but it is wonderful to see how his face falls when Batman interrupts his robbery of Van Jones at the end. In a way, Gorshin's manic Riddler laughter and his exuberant delight in his own successors make him arguably a better Joker-like villain than Romero's actual Joker performance. There is a moment in the 1966 *Batman* movie when the Joker and Riddler laugh in each other's faces, as if they are mirror images of each other.

Perhaps this, ultimately, is the reason why the TV series turned a Joker story from the comics into a Riddler story. Frank Gorshin's Riddler had become the funniest of the show's villains, the foremost example of the comedic trickster as criminal mastermind.

So it is unfortunate that "Death in Slow Motion" "The Riddler's False Notion" mark the end of Gorshin's great Riddler appearances on the *Batman* TV show. Gorshin memorably appeared in the 1966 movie alongside the other members of the TV show's Big Four villains, but the actor had salary disagreements with the show's producers and skipped the second season. This was, in itself, a factor in the show's decline in season two. The producers tried to work around Gorshin's absence by casting John Astin as the Riddler and apparently revamping a Riddler story into a vehicle for Maurice Evans as the Puzzler, but neither worked. Gorshin finally returned in the third and final season for a cameo in the first episode and a full guest villain appearance in the second, but then he vanished for the rest of the series. It is too bad in retrospect, but fans can be grateful for his great work as the Riddler in those eight episodes of the first season, all of them enduring classics.

Peter Sanderson is a comic book critic and historian, as well as an instructor/lecturer in the New York area concerning the study of graphic novels/comic books as literature. He is best known for his work as a researcher at the two main American comics companies, DC and Marvel, where he helped to catalog the various fictional characters that comprised their respective continuities.

Sanderson was also the writer of the *Marvel Saga* and *Wolverine Saga* limited series and an online column entitled Comics in Context, which (in Sanderson's own words) is "a weekly series of critical essays on comics, cartoon art, and related subjects" (those "related subjects" can run the gamut from film adaptations of comic books, to other media that have been influenced by comics, such as *Star Wars*). The series started on July 8, 2003 on the website IGN, but then moved to the Kevin Smith-affiliated website *Quick Stop Entertainment* on June 23, 2006. After a seventeen-month hiatus, Comics in Context returned to the newly rebranded A Site Called Fred on January 19, 2010

Outside of his online writings, Sanderson has also had a number of books published (including *The Marvel Vault* and *The Marvel Travel Guide to New York*), taught the class *The Graphic Novel as Literature* at New York University, curated an exhibition on Stan Lee for the Museum of Comic and Cartoon Art, and reviews the latest in comics and comics-related material for *Publishers Weekly*. In April 2017, he contributed a segment of a retrospective article on his late mentor, Mark Gruenwald for *Back Issue!* magazine #103. The segment focused on the academic and scholarly nature of Sanderson and Gruenwald's working relationship.

ZLONK!

The Last (?) Batman Adventure

"Fine Finny Fiends/Batman Makes the Scenes"
By Ed Catto

It wasn't a unique affliction then, and certainly isn't unique now. Simply put: I loved that *Batman* show.

The bat-zeitgeist splashed over those ½ hour episodic boundaries. I'd willingly embrace it each and every minute of each and every day. My wardrobe morphed into a bat-manifestation to such a degree that my mom had to repeatedly repair my terrycloth bat-cape. Clearly, the manufacturer never imagined it would be called into such intense crime-fighting service. My Marx pedal-powered Batmobile allowed me to commute to adventures from the living room all the way into the kitchen.

Throughout life, the adventure never really stopped. As a (supposed) adult, when I finally shared some time with Adam West, I incredulously realized how that meal may have been a "now-my-life-is-complete" moment.

My mania for Batman relegated me to a pop-culture island, patiently, yet diplomatically, tolerated by an uncomplaining wife, bemused relatives and supportive friends. My kids never got it, although I'd share (overshare?) Batman with them so many times in so many ways. For example, Cassie, my oldest daughter, was right there on the couch with me for the 1990s *Batman: The Animated Series* debut. I think she was more interested in the pancakes. My long-suffering mom and dad patiently supported my bat-fascination over the many, many years with a quiet, unconditional love that is a hallmark of truly spectacular parents.

Life is all about change. One fine day, my wife and I were shocked to find that we had become empty nesters. Our beloved town was tailor-made for raising kids, but we had outgrown it. So, we moved back to my hometown. As my parents still live here, we've been spending a lot of time with them. Their house is stuffed with momentos of lives well-lived. There is, as you'd expect, a bit of clutter. And every time we try to tame a new corner of Stately Catto Manor, we stumble upon unexpected treasures. We've found old matchbooks from Catskill hotels, vintage photographs with endearing smiles and prehistoric fashions, and Christmas decorations that surely must have been movie props. But the strangest thing we found was something my dad wrote in 1966. It was his reaction to two episodes of the *Batman* television show.

Dad is a bright, thoughtful guy. He was a leader in his field and penned a newspaper column for several years. As near as I can tell, this scrawled essay was his way of trying to make sense of that 1960s Batman phenomenon. It was written right after the first season's final episodes.

I'm eager to share it.

May 7, 1966

What a wild and strange thing *that* was. It's hard to believe that the *Batman* series burst onto the scene just a few months ago. I can still recall how that chilly January was warmed up with the colorful adventures of an old comic book hero. Jill Ireland in short shorts didn't hurt either.

The utter kookiness of *Batman*, christened Batmania by some, is still rampaging at full throttle. There are more and more Batman toys for sale. Those comics, of course, are still sold everywhere. The media is still sprinkling flourishes of the show into the national conversation – everything from "Holy This" or "Holy That" to the *POW! ZAPP! BIFF!* onomatopoeia.

They just aired the last two episodes of the *Batman* TV Show. Will it continue in the fall? I can't foretell the future. The closest thing to a crystal ball would be *TV Guide*'s "Fall TV Preview Issue", but that gets published in September.

It is true the *Batman* comic book has been going on for a while. At least I think it has. I sure wish there was some book or resource that cataloged all those old funny books. They were abundant when I was a kid. But nobody saves those old worthless magazines, so nobody really knows for sure when Batman's adventures started.

The way Hollywood plans for TV shows, and what is coming up next, is always a mystery to us all. Generally, it's a nice surprise. I think I read something about a *Batman* movie coming out this summer. But really, who is going to pay to go to a theater to see Batman, when the TV show aired for free? Even millionaires like Bruce Wayne (you probably don't know this, but that's Batman's real identity) don't have that kind of money to burn.

I'm not sure if there will be more Batman adventures after these end-of-the-season episodes. I think the gag has worn thin. I can't imagine that there are many more costumed hero stories left to tell. And obviously, while this comic hero is amusing now, everyone knows that in the future, funnybook stories could never be successful as movies or television programs. Beyond a few children, who would ever want to see them?

Besides, every Halloween some kid trick-or-treating in a Superman mask and cape is more than enough superheroes for us all.

I do have an idea, but I know it will never happen. I wish that Batman ran around with a girl instead of a teenage boy. It works for that Brit fellow on *The Avengers*, and I think that would be a good idea for this show. I know that the comic people would never let them recast Robin as a girl, so they should add a young woman to aid the Dynamic Duo. Maybe a Bat-Lady or a Bat-ette. Now *that* would really help expand the appeal *Batman*.

The Last Episodes of the Season

Although the character has taken over our house (my son Edward's enthusiasm is boundless), I haven't really sat down and watched a full Batman adventure story. After sitting through these last two episodes, I just had to get some of my thoughts down on paper. My wife Cassie just splurged and bought one of those new electronic pencil sharpeners, so writing this is so much easier than it would have been in the old days.

My son and I just watched the two-part *Batman* episodes where a bad guy, the Penguin, tried to steal money from millionaires. There was a lot going on and we both liked different aspects of it. Edward lives for the fight scenes. He also likes the leotards that Batman wears—I worry about that. I was surprised by, and smirked through, all the social commentary. *Batman* was filled with "winks" at the camera they must have slipped in as a reward for fathers like me. It's kind of like when Bob Hope turns to the camera in the middle of the movie, but a little more subtle.

Benevolent Millionaires

This tale may actually be a window into the inner workings of the very wealthy. It's interesting to see how the ultra-richest conduct their affairs. And it is a little scary to see how easy it would be for one criminal to undermine the system.

The basic premise of this episode is that the multi-millionaires of Gotham City will band together to decide upon one charity to which they will donate their millions.

The selection process seems odd, but I guess that's because I'm only a middle-class guy. All the multi-millionaires gather at a mansion of one particular multi-millionaire, (it is implied that this event rotates each year). Over cocktails and hors d'oeuvres, they "judge" each charity. To make the evaluation easier, each charity is represented by a model who parades around in a swimsuit and high heels.

Brilliant! I guess that's why these men became so successful. It's not so much that they were born into wealth, but they know how to make decisions better than the rest of us. These rich guys don't need old-fashioned time-consuming criteria. Elaborate reports detailing how funds get distributed? Nonsense! Extensive lists of a charity's successes, and failures, to determine the ability to achieve future goals? Forget it! A rundown of senior management, or board members, to better understand the caliber of the folks doing the work? Poppycock!

Their solution is so simple. Each charity, personified by a model in swimsuit, allows the millionaires to learn more over several cocktails through the night. There's obviously no need to worry about hanky-panky, because one millionaire's maiden aunt is at the party too. Models in swimsuits, an open bar, wealthy men...what could go wrong?

After one charity is chosen, they hold a *second* dinner party. For this event, the multi-millionaires each bring one million dollars to their subsequent soiree. (For security purposes, the location is undisclosed to the general public.) After dinner is served, a giant cake is wheeled out, from which one model, representing the selected charity, bursts out. The multi-millionaires throw their donations, in various denominations, at the model, while she poses in yet another swimsuit. Presumably, the multi-millionaires then find some servant to sweep up the bills and bring them to the charity's bank.

These episodes, by pulling back the curtain of the lives of the privileged, provide a rare glimpse for all the common rabble to understand the work that wealthy people undertake to keep charities afloat. How generous they are with not only their money, but with their time and austere judgment.

For this particular adventure, the nefarious Penguin has figured out how to beat the system. His plan is to ascertain the secret location of that second party (where the multi-millionaires throw the actual bills at the "cake girl") and steal the money strewn on the floor. Hmmm... *Oceans 11* this ain't!

The Penguin did have to do a little homework to prepare for this caper. First, he had to figure out where the dinner was to be held. Second, he had to determine which charity would be chosen. Spoiler Alert: (that phrase might catch on one day!) Miss Natural Resources (played by Lisa Mitchell) wins. She represents a charity that somehow does something positive with natural resources. Her title doesn't indicate her own natural resources. Or does it...? Third, the Penguin had to replace the actual Natural Resources model with his girlfriend (played by actress Julie Gregg). One other important item for his checklist: get sleeping gas to subdue the multi-millionaires at the banquet.

Come to think of it, just why did the Penguin have to replace Miss Natural Resources with his girlfriend? Wouldn't the sleep gas have just knocked out the winning charity model just like all the other millionaires and their servants?

A major plot element is the manner in which the Penguin deduces exactly where the multi-millionaires' dinner is to be held. It's a laborious process. The Penguin had to:

1. Create a phony pop-up fish storefront
2. Lure millionaire Bruce Wayne's butler there to buy the caviar (one pound per millionaire!) for the first dinner party
3. Subdue the butler
4. Brainwash the butler so that he would reveal the secret party location
5. Check in with the butler periodically because he didn't know the secret address at the time of abduction
6. Fulfill the butler's fish and caviar orders for the dinner party, so no one realizes there's trouble afoot - an inglorious task for a criminal mastermind to be sure

Again, to a regular guy like me that plan seems pretty complicated! But Batman is a sharp observer of human nature, and he notices that something is amiss with his butler. I think that, as the story goes, this butler also became his surrogate parent after the tragic death of Wayne's parents.

I can't help but think that Batman had *so many other ways* to thwart this crime:

- He could have just asked the multi-millionaires to write checks to the charity.
- He could have arranged for the funds to be transferred electronically. (And then just used play money to throw at the model, in order to continue the millionaire's misogynist tradition.)
- He could have asked the Gotham Police to stand guard during the dinner.
- He could have requested the Gotham Police raid the Penguin's lair.

But why should the multi-millionaires have to change their plans? These wealthy fellows are already working *so hard* to give their money away, why should they *also* have to be asked to change their longstanding traditions of cocktailing with swimsuit models?

In fact, I bet in the future that industry leaders, and maybe even presidents, will actually run beauty contests.

Batman and Robin anticipate the Penguin's schemes and prepare a sting operation. So...as planned by the Penguin, the multi-millionaires are rendered unconscious by sleeping gas at that second dinner. One multi-millionaire, Bruce Wayne was out of town. No eyebrows are raised, because wealthy types, I expect, do that all the time. And besides, he ended up throwing a *third* party (at the end of the show) to make up for the debacle of the entrapment.

Is this show meant to be a commentary on how millionaire Bruce Wayne helps all the common folk? In his Batman identity, he is unencumbered by the little the things that plague the rest of us (traffic rules, laws about trespassing and/or breaking & entering, due process, etc.). But if he didn't develop the elaborate Batman persona, complete with a car, a subterranean secret headquarters and special weapons, the existing infrastructure designed to keep Gotham citizens safe clearly would fail.

Redemption and Kindness

Seriously, though, one thing that comes through loud and clear is Batman's kindness. He's the smartest guy in the room and three steps ahead of everybody. But curiously, he's not a know-it-all.

Other superheroes like Superman and that new guy, Spider-Man, have powers and abilities far beyond mortal men. Batman and Robin, on the other hand, are just regular guys who train really hard and leverage their enormous wealth for the greater good. Curiously, the outstanding abilities that Batman showed in these episodes were super-encouragement and kindness. For example:

- When surrounded by the inept senior management of the Gotham City Police force, Batman never diminishes their mediocre accomplishments. On the contrary—he lauds their feeble efforts.
- When mentoring his faithful ward, Dick Grayson, who is secretly Robin the Boy Wonder, it's clear Batman already has all the answers. But he lays out the clues so his pal Robin can solve each puzzle himself. As a mentor, Batman even transforms small opportunities, like crossing the street, into teaching moments.
- When dealing with other millionaires, when he's secretly planning to thwart the Penguin's plans, he still finds time to be polite.

He's kind to his employees too. One of the other multi-millionaires chews on his hors d'oeuvres and finds, to his surprise, he's bitten into a fishhook. Apparently, it fell into the food from Alfred's overcoat! But Bruce Wayne doesn't publicly rebuke his butler. There's no need and clearly Alfred accepted the responsibility for this potentially disastrous mishap. Bruce Wayne would never scream "You're Fired!" to an employee, and I'm sure successful wealthy people of the future will never do that.

At the conclusion of the adventure, Bruce Wayne graciously treats the Penguin's girlfriend, who had colluded to murder Batman and steal millions, with patience and kindness. Maybe it was because she showed up as Commissioner Gordon's date. Surely, he's not a multi-millionaire too? Or maybe she just looked good wrapped in that fur. Perhaps that is standard operating procedure for felons in Gotham City.

I can't help but wonder: is this whole Batman operation a good use of funds? The car, the cave, the computers? Bruce Wayne sure is writing out some big checks. Wouldn't it have been more efficient, instead of bankrolling the Batman operation, to just have taken all that money, paid the Penguin a million and donated the rest to charity?

Fight Club

I don't remember the world ever getting this goofy about a TV show. Oh, sure, I liked *Hopalong Cassidy* quite a bit back in the day, but this show has affected my boy, Edward, in a big way.

He wears that terry cloth bat-cape so much that my wife always has to repairs the straps. And whenever he's with his little pals, they jump around on the furniture like over-caffeinated maniacs in an elaborate ballet full of roundhouse punches, leaps and kicks.

Several things about these episodes still don't make sense to me. In that first episode, I was surprised to find Batman and Robin subdued by the Penguin and his two thugs. Aren't the Dynamic Duo supposed to be trained for this type of confrontation?

At least the Penguin's helpers had the good manners not to use real-life tools of the trade during this fight. I don't think my boy was ready to see Robin and Batman outwit pistols, knives, brass knuckles or black-jacks.

After the Dynamic Duo was captured, I wonder why the nefarious Penguin didn't pull off their masks? Where's the criminal's curiosity? And the Penguin would surely have known the face of Millionaire Bruce Wayne, as his hosting the multi-millionaires party was such an integral part of this caper. Maybe the Penguin already knows Batman's true identity? Are the writers implying that everyone in Gotham City already knows that Batman is Bruce Wayne and they all just indulge the wealthy lunatic?

In this adventure, the Penguin's girlfriend didn't get involved at all in the fights, despite being in the middle of the action. An obsessive narcissist, she preened and posed in front of a mirror the whole time, evaluating and adjusting her swimsuits. It seemed incongruent to me that she'd be so oblivious to the battle at hand, but given just how interesting that swimsuit looked, maybe it does made sense. I'd have preferred to focus on her in the swimsuit than Batman in his leotards, if I am to be completely honest.

Like all these little trends, I know that my boy will soon focus on the normal things, like football. I expect these Batman fight scenes will evaporate from his memory soon. In a year or two, who will even remember the *POW! BAM! KER-SPLATT* nonsense?

In Color

This show is broadcast in color and that is a big part of its success. We weren't the first family in town to upgrade to a color TV, but I'm really glad we did. In the future, I wonder if all shows will be filmed in color? Luckily, the reception is pretty good around here. It does fuzz out when we run the blender or when my wife gives the boy an electric-razor haircut.

I think that after five months of the *Batman* show, all of America is used to the Caped Crusader's colorful uniform, the Penguin's purple hat, and the high-gloss and red striping of the Batmobile. During this particular escapade, they've spiced it up with models in color swimsuits. One time the Penguin's girlfriend even wears powder blue go-go boots. Another reward for all the dads who have suffered through show since January.

The cliffhanger moment at the end of the first episode is colorful too. It has something to do with sucking the pressure out of a chamber in which Batman and Robin are tied up. The tension of the impending doom is illustrated as colorful balloons pop, one by one. As each balloon pops, the life-sustaining air pressure in the room decreases. Colorful or not, I just didn't get it. Whatever happened to the days of spiked walls closing in on the hero? Or did they do that one already?

Changing the Channel

Batman does make me smile, but there are so many other good shows on TV. I am sure they will last longer and be the programs that people remember.

F-Troop is more about the world I know—where everyone has an angle and is gaming the system. The "hero" of the story, the fort's captain, is really a bumbling idiot, manipulated by both his second-in-command and the nearby Indian tribes. Kind of like the real world I live in. Too often, the real world is more *Sgt. Bilko* than *Sgt. Preston.*

This Batman thing seems to have replaced two shows that my wife and I really liked.

One was *The Adventures of Ozzie* and Harriet. Before TV, I remember listening to this on the radio and even read (and traded) a comic about Ozzie and Harriet. Even though I grew up in an Italian-American family, I could relate to this family. We were never as squeaky clean as the Nelsons, but I am sure my mom is a better cook than Harriet Nelson. She's so good, in fact that, that she makes the meatballs for three of the local restaurants here in town.

The other show we liked was the polar opposite: a music show called *Shindig!* For a music lover like me (I actually owned a pair of blue suede shoes in high school) this was a real treat. Every week, they'd show bands performing their newest songs. Maybe one day in the future, someone with a little foresight will invent an entire TV channel dedicated to showing short films of bands performing songs.

The really strange part of it, of course, is that in the future everyone will remember both *Shindig!* and *Ozzie and Harriet*, while the trendy TV *Batman* show will surely be forgotten and relegated to some footnote in a "History of TV" book on some dusty library shelf.

Now that I think about it, there are some strange shows debuting recently: *The Munsters, Lost in Space, Star Trek.* They all are so forgettable. It's easy to realize that the normal shows on TV right now, like *Mona McClusky* (with the dancer Juliet Prowse) and *The Loner*, created by *The Twilight Zone*'s Rod Serling, will be the ones that will live on forever.

The Return of Batman?

Will there be more *Batman* episodes? Trends usually burn out quickly. Like the man says, all we can do to find out is tune into that same Bat-Channel in the fall. It will be nice to get rid of all the Batman toys and comics when my son grows out of it. After all, who needs to keep all this worthless stuff when you can get two or three bucks for it a garage sale?

Bill Catto
Auburn, NY
May 1966

Although he's outgrown his terry cloth bat-cape, **Ed Catto** continues to read, collect and write about Batman, comics and pop culture for *Pop Culture Squad*, *Back Issue Magazine*, the *Overstreet Comic Book Price Guide* and *ComicMix*. His art reflects the influence of and appreciation for the great comic and pulp illustrators. Employing traditional sketching and inking techniques, he was voted "Best Interior Artist" for the 2018 Pulp Factory Awards. Having recently returned to the Finger Lakes Region, Ed has joined the faculty of Ithaca College's School of Business and founded Agendae, a a strategic marketing firm. Between consulting, writing, teaching and drawing, Ed continues to work very hard to whittle down the teetering tower of books on his nightstand.

ZOWIE!

Yo Ho! Batman Goes Theatrical and (Kind of) Political

Batman Feature Film
By Rich Handley

It's commonplace nowadays for television shows to make a jump to the silver screen. Back in 1966, however, it was practically unheard of—especially while a show was still airing new episodes. This makes the *Batman* feature film rather unique in cinematic history.

A continuation of the Caped Crusaders' campy televised exploits, the film stars Adam West and Burt Ward as Batman and Robin, with Cesar Romero as the Joker, Frank Gorshin as the Riddler, Burgess Meredith as the Penguin, and Lee Meriwether replacing Julie Newmar as Catwoman. Writer Lorenzo Semple Jr., director Leslie H. Martinson, and producer William Dozier crafted a whimsical take on Bob Kane's masked crime-fighting duo, but viewed through the lens of the real-world politics of the 1960s, the movie takes on added meaning. Several aspects of its plot—the dispensing of war-surplus submarines, the mishandling of Polaris solid-fueled nuclear-armed ballistic missiles, the failure of diplomats to achieve meaningful peace talks, and so forth—reflect the era in which the movie was made.

The 1960s were the height of the Cold War, a period of geopolitical tension between the United Sates and the Union of Soviet Socialist Republics, and many feared that a global thermonuclear war might result in mutual annihilation. The film has been dubbed a satire, both of Batman and of the superhero genre, but it also turned a critical eye toward the U.S. government's activities. *Batman: The Movie* was silly fun, but in its own way, it was topically relevant to the issues dominating the headlines of the era.

Of course, political commentary is merely one of the film's many facets, and hardly the most paramount. This is *Batman*, after all—not *Wag the Bat.*

The 1966 film has aspects in common with the Batman movies that followed, and with those that had preceded it. Like 1949's *Batman and Robin*, starring Robert Lowery, it sees Batman brandishing an amusing crime-fighting weapon: a can of Shark Repellent Bat-Spray, as absurd as the full-sized oxy-acetylene torch Lowery somehow pulls from his belt. Like 1989's *Batman*, it stars a non-imposing actor (Michael Keaton) who is surprisingly effective in the title role. And like 1992's *Batman Returns* (Keaton again), it teams up Catwoman and the Penguin in a rather contrived plot—and the Penguin steals the Batmobile in both stories.

As with 1995's *Batman Forever* (Val Kilmer) and 1997's *Batman & Robin* (George Clooney), *Batman* favors the campy TV approach to humor. Plus, it combines the efforts of four villains (Clooney's film features Jason Woodrue, Poison Ivy, Mister Freeze, and Bane), though West's film does a far better job on that front. The movie has less in common with Christopher Nolan's darker Batman trilogy starring Christian Bale, recent movies featuring Ben Affleck, or the *Gotham* TV show starring David Mazouz. However, it *does* see the Caped Crusader risk his life to remove a large bomb from a populated area of Gotham City, which plays out again (albeit not for laughs) in *The Dark Knight Rises.*

What about 1943's *Batman*, starring Lewis Wilson, you ask? Although that serial bears little resemblance to 1966's *Batman*, it has a unique connection that goes beyond surface similarities, in that Wilson's adventure inspired the latter's creation. How so? Well, in 1965, the complete serial returned to theaters under the title *An Evening with Batman and Robin*. The re-release proved so successful that it ushered in a new era of Batmania, enabling West's comedic series to hit the airwaves the following year.

Released between the TV show's first two seasons, the movie had a built-in audience, though that was not originally the plan. Dozier had intended the movie to predate the TV series and serve as an interest-generating pilot, but financial considerations got in the way, with 20th Century Fox opting to share costs with a television studio rather than footing the bill itself. As a result, the West-Ward Dynamic Duo debuted in viewers' living rooms rather than at the cinema.

The credits offer poetic acknowledgments scrawled on a brick wall, viewed through a police search light: "We wish to express our gratitude to the enemies of crime and crusaders against crime throughout the world for their inspirational example. To them, and to lovers of adventure, lovers of pure escapism, lovers of unadulterated entertainment, lovers of the ridiculous and the bizarre—to fun-lovers everywhere—this picture is respectfully dedicated." The camera briefly pans to two lovers locked in a passionate embrace, then the acknowledgments conclude: "If we have overlooked any sizable groups of lovers, we apologize. —The Producers"

"Ridiculous and bizarre," indeed! Those acknowledgments are positively weird. As the search-light credits continue, Batman, Robin, and the movies' villains take turns mugging for the camera, as though consciously aware they're fictional characters in a campy superhero yarn. Finally, as Batman and Robin drive off in the Batmobile, a trench-coated thug runs across town in a sped-up manner before stopping to check out a cigarette-smoking prostitute standing in a doorway. (No, seriously.)

This is clearly not a Tim Burton Batman movie. It's not a Chris Nolan Batman movie. Heck, it's not even a Joel Schumacher Batman movie… though it is, at times, close. It's a Leslie Martinson Batman movie, and it's doing bat-things in its own damn bat-way, accompanied by a wonderfully jazzy 1960s bat-soundtrack by Nelson Riddle—who, by virtue of his last name, was surely destined from birth to score a Batman series.

As the story opens, Bruce Wayne and Dick Grayson investigate the disappearance of Commodore Schmidlapp, a clueless inventor who has no idea he, his yacht, and his genius invention (a matter dehydrator and rehydrator) have been abducted by the United Underworld—the combined forces of those four diabolical evildoers, the Joker, the Catwoman, the Riddler, and the Penguin.

Just how clueless is Schmidlapp? For starters, he finds nothing unusual about his chortling steward wearing a garish purple suit and clown makeup that fails to hide a thick mustache, not to mention said steward looking exactly like a known super-criminal. Furthermore, despite his having lived life at sea, it's remarkably easy to trick the commodore, using a fog machine and sound effects, into believing he's sailing the ocean blue and not being held hostage in an evil lair. One can't help but wonder how such a man could invent anything more complex than candy-corn fangs.

Batman and Robin contact an airport, where a slew of personnel (apparently on standby, waiting for the Dynamic Duo to require their services) ready the Batcopter. Who pays the fees for hangar storage, labor, and maintenance, since no one knows the Caped Crusaders' identities in order to bill them? Perhaps Batman charges them to his GothCard credit card, from Schumacher's *Batman & Robin*. Perhaps the city covers the expense. Or maybe *no one* pays the fees, which would explain why the copter wasn't used in the TV show's later seasons—the vessel had been impounded for non-payment.

The duo fly to the commodore's yacht, where Batman descends a well-labeled "bat ladder," only to discover that the boat is a projected mirage, with the not-so-Dark Knight dangling hip-deep in the ocean. A shark that in no way looks like a fake rubber movie prop bloodlessly chomps Batman's leg all the way up to his knee, puncturing neither his skin nor even his tights with its razor-sharp teeth. As Batman bops the beast repeatedly about the head and ribs, Robin climbs down the ladder at a pace that is weirdly leisurely, given the situation's urgency. The Boy Wonder then executes a midair upside-down turn that is more awkward and tentative than one might expect from someone raised in a family of circus performers.

Robin hands his mentor a can of Shark Repellent Bat-Spray from a rack containing "Oceanic Repellent Bat Sprays" for warding off barracudas, whales, manta rays, and sharks, enabling Batman to rid himself of his faux-finned foe. This begs the question of how often the Dynamic Duo find themselves attacked by barracudas, whales, manta rays, and sharks, that they would need to equip the Batcopter with protections from such specific animals—not to mention how helpless they would be if, say, a giant squid, a manatee, or an angry clam were to accost them with no appropriate repellants available. In any case, Robin and his astoundingly uninjured companion watch in horror as the pepper-sprayed animal drops back to the sea—and promptly explodes upon impact.

At a later press conference, journalists question Batman regarding the vanishing yacht and the incendiary shark. Rather than telling them what had transpired, Batman takes a page from the political playbook and neatly sidesteps their queries, openly lying and providing no useful information whatsoever. It's a bit disappointing to see Batman, a hero sworn to protect the people and uphold justice, treating the media so cavalierly. In an era marked by political activism against injustice and fascism, a growing distrust of rigid authority, and a movement away from social constraints toward greater individual freedoms and governmental accountability, you'd think someone like Batman would recognize the importance of having a free and unencumbered press.

Ah, but then, Bruce Wayne *is* a member of the one percent, after all.

Chief O'Hara fares just as poorly as an upholder of the U.S.

Constitution. He chastises the reporters, saying they should consider themselves *lucky* the heroes are talking to them *at all*, which shows how little regard the blatant Irish stereotype has for law-enforcement transparency and freedom of the press. Or maybe he's just disgusted that one fake-news journalist mispronounced the commodore's name as "Smithlapp," due to an actor's flubbed line making the final cut.

Attending the press conference is Catwoman, cleverly disguised as Soviet reporter Miss Kitka. The filmmakers' decision to have Catwoman pretend to be Russian was subtle but significant. In the mid-1960s, relations between the United States and the U.S.S.R. were on the verge of eruption. The U-2 Incident of 1960, in which a U.S. reconnaissance jet was shot down while flying over Soviet territory, was followed by the 1961 Berlin Crisis, during which President John F. Kennedy activated 150,000 reservists and warned Americans about the threat of a Soviet attack. This led to the Cuban Missile Crisis in 1962, which very nearly resulted in all-out nuclear war. The subsequent establishment of a U.S.-Soviet hotline and the Limited Test Ban Treaty helped to ease tensions between the nations, but distrust of anything Soviet would continue to fester.

Kitka's Russian accent thus carried a lot of meaning for 1966 film-goers, as it earmarked her as someone about whom the audience should be immediately suspicious. Regardless, Batman grows smitten with her Natasha Fatale accent and is charmed rather than miffed when she compares him and Robin to masked Western vigilantes—which the apoplectic O'Hara and Commissioner Gordon find outlandish and scandalizing, but is actually a pretty accurate description of the Dynamic Duo, all things considered.

Following the perfunctory pretense at a press palaver, the caped crime-fighters and their policemen pals take a Möbius strip-like leap of logic and conclude that Catwoman, the Joker, the Penguin, and the Riddler must have joined forces. How do they figure this out without any evidence that might reasonably lead to such a realization? Well, the shark incident was "pretty fishy," like a penguin. It happened at sea, which sounds like "C" for "cat." The shark was pulling Batman's leg—a joke. And it all adds up to a sinister riddle.

Now *that* is stellar police work.

Kitka returns to the United Underworld's lair, where the villains demonstrate remarkable team work. Not only do they have a cool logo, a menacing motto ("Today Gotham City—Tomorrow the World"), and a team of loyal henchmen, but they've agreeably divided their shelves into four separately labeled sections to store riddles, jokes, penguin food, and catnip. That's pretty impressive! Despite clearly despising each other, these four egomaniacs have found a way to work past their differences and function as a single criminal entity with a "share and share alike" mentality.

This makes them far more effective a team than the United World Organization (a clear United Nations analogue), whose members fail to make any decisions or even notice they're being kidnapped; Gotham City's police force, who are utterly useless without Batman saving the day; or President Lyndon B. Johnson, who sits in the Oval Office doing absolutely nothing about a rogue submarine lurking in nearby coastal waters. What's more, despite being greedy, violent, and criminally insane, they have a remarkable ability to self-regulate and stay on target whenever the inclination to argue amongst themselves rears its colorfully costumed head. Consider the following dialogue:

CATWOMAN: United Underworld. Tch. We're about as united as the members of the United World headquarters on Gotham East River. What's the *matter* with you all?

RIDDLER: She's right. She's right—if we don't manage to somehow swallow our super-criminal pride, I'm afraid we'll—

PENGUIN: Right, Mister Riddler. Quite right. We must hang together, or most assuredly, we shall hang separately.

JOKER: Oh, and what a pity that would be on the eve of the greatest criminal coup anyone ever dreamed of!

Quite a team, eh? If the filmmakers were intentionally commenting on how poorly run governments tend to be compared to how well criminal organizations manage their operations, the message is clear—and it's just as applicable to the modern political scene as it was in the era of miniskirts and beehive haircuts. If only the U.S. Congress could set aside its pesky partisan politics and accomplish even half as much as the United Underworld does, we might all have our own priceless collections of Etruscan snoods.

Incidentally, Johnson's ineffectiveness in the film is surprising, as the ex-President has historically been described as a tireless, ruthlessly effective politician who worked long hours, had a knack for seeing legislation passed, and was passionate about eliminating poverty and racial injustice, as evidenced by his "Great Society" programs. Here, however, he just sits back and lets Batman prevent the Apocalypse. Perhaps in a world in which masked vigilantes have the support of the public and law-enforcement alike, the political climate might be sufficiently altered that it would curtail Presidential usefulness. Or it could simply be that the filmmakers were angry about Johnson's decision, in March 1965, to commit U.S. combat ground troops to aid South Vietnam in its war against the Soviet-assisted Viet Cong, and thus portrayed him unfavorably.

In any event, the United Underworld's plot is clever and appropriately wacky: they plan to use Schmidlapp's dehydrating machine to turn world leaders into dust and hold them for ransom, like a quartet of demented Ernst Blofelds. This convoluted plot involves repeated attempts to eliminate Batman and Robin, first with the exploding shark, then with Polaris missiles and an exploding octopus; keeping Schmidlapp blissfully unaware he's in captivity, and not on a cruise ship; and sneaking dehydrated pirate henchmen, who yell "Yo ho!" at the drop of a hat, into the Batcave.

Throughout all this mayhem and thinly veiled political pseudo-commentary, Adam West masterfully manages to remain serious and credible while spouting ridiculous lines in equally ridiculous scenarios. The dangers that the Dynamic Duo face are absurd (being magnetically stuck to an ocean buoy, for instance), as are their solutions to the problems (such as "reversing the polarity," a phrase later popularized on *Star Trek* and *Doctor Who*). Only West could pull off a line like "Confound it! The batteries are dead!" without seeming lampoonish. No matter how silly the situation and script might become, West maintains his dignity, even while being in on the gag.

The same can be said for Burt Ward, who with absolute solemnity recites lines like "Gosh, Batman, the nobility of the almost-human porpoise" and "Banana... Russian... I've got it! Someone Russian is going to slip on a banana peel and break their neck!" and "It looks bad, Batman. This brassy bird has us buffaloed!" An ideal straight man, Ward sets up West's sober reply to the porpoise comment ("True, Robin. It was noble of that animal to hurl himself into the path of that final torpedo. He gave his life for ours."). Likewise, Batman's response to Robin's banana-peel statement ("Precisely Robin—the *only* possible meaning.") somehow seems entirely reasonable, despite there being *any number* of other possible meanings to the villains' vague clues that would be far more likely than someone stepping on a fruit skin and suffering a vertebral fracture.

It's this that ensures the film's most iconic scene, involving Batman's attempt to save Gotham's inhabitants from an oversized fuse-lit bomb, never goes so far into farce as to ruin the movie. The sight of Batman hoofing it around a seaport, desperately trying to find a place to throw the explosive device, only to run into a marching band, tavern riffraff, nuns, a mother and infant, young lovers (the ones referenced in the opening acknowledgments, perhaps?), a family of ducks, and others whom he refuses to endanger, is hilarious. But it's the exasperation in Batman's voice as he observes, "Some days, you just can't get rid of a bomb!" that truly sells it. Ask anyone if they've ever watched the Batman movie from the 1960s, and chances are good they'll respond, "Isn't that the one where he can't get rid of the bomb?"

Equally amusing is a scene in which Batman, upon discovering the existence of a flipper-flapping submarine, calls the U.S. Navy to chastise goofy Vice Admiral Fangschliester—who is playing tiddlywinks with his adorable assistant instead of doing any actual work (a clear condemnation of the U.S. military's irresponsible blunders in the 1960s)—for allowing such a dangerous weapon to fall into the hands of a criminal:

ADMIRAL: Hello, Batman. Ahoy! What can I do for you?

BATMAN: Hello, Admiral. A routine question. Have you recently sold any war-surplus submarines? And if so, to whom?

ADMIRAL: Just a moment, I'll have to look that up. [*Checks a Rolodex, whistling cheerfully.*] Answer: affirmative, Batman. We disposed of a war-surplus submarine last Friday… a pre-atomic model… to some chap named P.N. Gwynne.

BATMAN: P.N. Gwynne?

ROBIN: The Penguin!

BATMAN: Did this P.N. Gwynne leave an address?

ADMIRAL: No, just a Post Office box number. Would you like it?

BATMAN: No, thank you, Admiral. You've been very helpful.

ADMIRAL: Avast and belay, Batman. Your tone sounds rather grim. We haven't done anything *foolish*, have we?

BATMAN: Disposing of pre-atomic submarines to persons who don't even leave their full addresses? [*Pause.*] Good day, Admiral.

Fangschliester's cheerful demeanor and absurd phrasings, juxtaposed with Batman's disapproving tone, provide a rather harsh mockery of the U.S. military's leadership. The admiral's idiocy and juvenile game-playing spotlight the folly of the government's lack of foresight and oversight in arming those who would later attack the United States using its own weapons. Consider the World Trade Center's September 2001 destruction by *mujahideen* militants whom the U.S. government had armed to fight the Soviet Union during the Soviet-Afghan War. As ridiculous as it may sound, the Penguin here becomes Batman's Osama Bin Laden.

But it isn't just the non-subtle social commentary or the well-timed, wonderfully self-aware humor that makes the 1966 *Batman* so enjoyable. The film is more than merely a parody, after all, and reducing it to sight gags and one-liners would do it a grave injustice. No, what makes the movie worthwhile is the sheer joy with which Burgess Meredith, Cesar Romero, and especially Frank Gorshin reprise the characters they'd made famous during the weekly series' freshman season. Barely hidden Joker mustaches aside, these three actors are fan favorites, and deservedly so. Meredith's waddle, squint, and bird-like laugh evoke actual penguins with every movement and utterance, while Romero's infectious cackle has become a hallmark of the character, matched only by Mark Hamill's psychotic giggling on *Batman: The Animated Series* and Joaquin Phoenix's discomforting outbursts of pained hilarity in 2019's *Joker*.

Meanwhile, Gorshin's version of the Riddler, equal parts cold anger and barely contained giddiness, transforms a minor comic book villain of that era into arguably the show's best criminal character. It's no wonder Jim Carrey would later channel Gorshin's approach in *Batman Forever*. One would be hard-pressed not to burst out laughing while watching the Riddler dance around like a coked-up asylum patient, singing "I know the perfect victim! I know the perfect victim!"—before suddenly snapping to a cold, calm demeanor and suggesting Kitka lure Batman into a trap by seducing Bruce Wayne.

Romero and Gorshin are each brilliant on their own, but together, they make a delightful team. During the movie's final act, the Joker tries to stop the Riddler from wasting time sending the Caped Crusaders "crazy clues," but the sugar-rushed lunatic, practically bouncing off the submarine walls with orgasmic glee, crows, "But I must! I must! Oh, outwitting Batman is my sole delight, my joy, my Heaven on Earth—my very paradise!" This is one of the movie's best-delivered speeches, and it's perfectly complemented by the exasperated stare on the Joker's face. It's a shame the writers didn't give these two actors more opportunities to play off each other's strengths.

Notice that Lee Meriwether's Catwoman is absent from the above praise. That's not a condemnation of Meriwether's acting skills, for she's a fine performer and might have been better in the role had she been able to make it her own. Unfortunately, she had the misfortune of following in the footsteps of the incomparably glamorous Julie Newmar, whose every breath, syllable, and movement during her season-one appearances oozed feline seductiveness. In attempting to channel Newmar's quintessential and nuanced approach, Meriwether comes up short by comparison, making her the least interesting of the film's four villains and the least memorable of the West era's three Catwomen. Consider the commanding performances of both Michelle Pfeiffer and Anne Hathaway in later films, and it's easy to see that Meriwether is basically just Newmar-Lite.

The result is wasted potential. The Bruce-Kitka romance falls slightly flat—through no fault of West, who throws himself into the scenes with love-struck gusto. West may be good as Batman, but he is *great* as his alter-ego Bruce Wayne, and he upstages her in their scenes together (as do her male villainous counterparts). Imagine how sensual the already sexualized dialogue discussing Bruce's dreams of Kitka approaching a "climax" might have been had he been playing opposite the purr-fect Ms. Newmar! Thankfully, Newmar again portrayed Catwoman in *Batman*'s second season, while Eartha Kitt, not Meriwether, was hired when Newmar proved unavailable to return for season three. With no disrespect meant to Meriwether, it was a wise decision. Just ask Wong Foo.

Batman is ensnared in the United Underworld's trap and is taken to their lair. Unaware that Kitka and Catwoman are the same person, he vows, "I swear by Heaven, if you harm that girl, I'll *kill you all.* I'll rend you limb from limb!" The next time you hear someone condemn the Burton or Nolan films by claiming Batman never kills, remind them of this scene. Perhaps it will help to dispel this long-held fan misconception.

Eventually, the villains stop futzing about with detonating sea-life, kidnapping millionaires, and firing a seemingly endless supply of Polaris missiles at Batman, and finally put into motion their actual plan: reducing the United World Organization's Security Council to technicolor powder piles, to be ransomed for nine billion dollars in cash. The Dynamic Duo thwart this plot with a hearty bout of fisticuffs at sea, during which the villains and their henchmen take turns being punched or kicked off the side of the submarine (oddly, the Riddler takes a plunge *twice*). After cowering for the duration of the melee, Catwoman impressively knocks both Batman and Robin over the side, then she, too, is dispatched by… er… tripping over a clearly visible obstacle.

Our heroes save the powdered diplomats, though Schmidlapp clumsily shatters the vials containing them and idiotically sneezes on their spilled contents (seriously, how did this guy ever invent *anything*?). Batman separates the dust by "ethnic and national factors," though it's unclear why this would be necessary since each person's dust is a different bright Play-Doh-like color. Robin drives home the film's social commentary by suggesting, "With the way the world is and all... don't you think maybe we ought to try to improve those factors? Kind of reshuffle them a little?" Yet despite having never watched a single *Jurassic Park* film, Batman takes a cue from Jeff Goldblum, telling his young ward, "No, it's not for mortals like us to tamper with the laws of nature."

Awed by such bat-wisdom, Robin can't help but agree.

Still, the rehydration process proves imperfect, with the recombined councilors swapping native languages, and thus cultural perspectives. Amazingly, not one of them is immediately impaled on the long metal rehydration tubes on their chairs, which should surely have pierced their internal organs and spines the moment their bodies re-formed. Seemingly unaware that any of this has happened—or that Batman, Robin, and the police are now in the room—the diplomats continue the tiresome squabbling in which they'd been engaged before being turned into Pixy Stix. The United Nations has frequently been criticized for its members' failure to move past differing ideologies and accomplish anything meaningful, and the parallel here is right on the bat-nose.

Surveying the botched results, Batman rationalizes his failure to put all the king's men back together again: "Who knows, Robin? This strange mixing of minds may be the greatest single service ever performed for humanity." Sure, it's ham-fisted moralizing and more than a little nonsensical, but West delivers the line with grace and charisma, leaving 1960s viewers to ponder, as Batman and Robin sneak out a window before anyone can call them on their shoddy workmanship, whether mankind could rise above petty international disputes and avoid the movie's cryptic final warning of "The living end"—a phrase denoting an extreme example of any given scenario, which can be used both positively and pejoratively. In the case of the film's conclusion, both are apropos.

Sadly, the world has failed to learn the lessons of the *Batman* feature film. The U.S.S.R. may no longer exist, but Russia still dominates headlines as a political enemy of the United States. Mutual annihilation thankfully hasn't occurred, but nuclear weapons are still a major threat, with North Korea upping the ante, and with the suspension of the Intermediate-Range Nuclear Forces Treaty—a pact with Russia that had helped to maintain European security since the Cold War—in 2019. News headlines are replete with reports of police, military, and government officials making bad decisions due to an appalling lack of foresight and oversight on the part of modern-day Fangschliesters. And while real-world evil-doers don't blatantly advertise themselves with brightly colored costumes, wild makeup, and crazed cackling, we do have our fair share of villains.

If only Batman were here to clean up the place.

Rich Handley edits Eaglemoss's *Star Trek: The Graphic Novel Collection* and has written the introductions to most volumes of that series. He has written books about *Planet of the Apes*, *Back to the Future*, and *Watchmen*, as well as licensed *Star Wars* and *Planet of the Apes* fiction. Rich co-edited Titan's Scribe Award-nominated *Planet of the Apes: Tales from the Forbidden Zone* with Jim Beard, plus eight Sequart anthologies to date discussing *Planet of the Apes*, *Star Wars*, *Battlestar Galactica*, *Hellblazer*, and classic monsters. He has written for DC's *Hellblazer: 30th Anniversary Celebration*; IDW's five *Star Trek* and three Eisner Award-nominated *Star Wars* comic-strip reprint hardcovers; BOOM! Studios' four-volume *Planet of the Apes Archive* series; Sequart anthologies about *Star Trek*, *Blade Runner*, and *Back to the Future*; and ATB Publishing's Outside In series focused on *Star Trek*, *Buffy the Vampire Slayer*, *Angel*, and *The X-Files*. In addition, Rich is a weekly columnist for HeroCollector.com and the managing editor of RFIDJournal.com.

ACKNOWLEDGMENTS

The editor would like to acknowledge the contributions of several people, without which this book wouldn't have made it to the finish line:

Rich Handley
Ed Catto
Sean Dulaney
Keith Howell
Robert Long
Matt Orsman

And…tune in again, some Bat-time,
same Bat-publisher for:

BIFF! BAM! EEE-YOW!

The Subterranean Blue Grotto Essays on Batman '66 – Season Two

The best is yet to come!

www.ingramcontent.com/pod-product-compliance
Ingram Content Group UK Ltd.
Pitfield, Milton Keynes, MK11 3LW, UK
UKHW012249290726
14090UKWH00013B/551

9 798474 623429